D0223102

Praise for *The Happiness Plan*

"Filled with Camel McConnell's motivating energy and her affirming and realistic approach to life, this book can and will change lives."

Kim Price, Head of Extended Services, Millfields Community School, and Children's Centre, Hackney

"Carmel McConnell is one of these people who has the amazing knack of helping you see that *you* are in charge of your life and therefore *you* have the possibility to make it better. *The Happiness Plan* offers practical, compelling advice spoken from the heart."

Anna MacLean, Marketing Manager, (Inbev UK Ltd)

THE HAPPINESS PLAN

Prentice Hall LIFE

If life is what you make it, then making it better starts here.

What we learn today can change our lives tomorrow. It can change our goals or change our minds; open up new opportunities or simply inspire us to make a difference. That's why we have created a new breed of books that do more to help you make more of *your* life.

Whether you want more confidence or less stress, a new skill or a different perspective, we've designed *Prentice Hall Life* books to help you to make a change for the better. Together with our authors we share a commitment to bring you the brightest ideas and best ways to manage your life, work and wealth.

In these pages we hope you'll find the ideas you need for the life *you* want. Go on, help yourself.

It's what you make it

* * *

THE HAPPINESS PLAN

Simple steps to a happier life

Carmel McConnell

Harlow, England • London • New York • Boston • San Francisco • Toronto • Sydney • Singapore • Hong Kong
Tokyo • Seoul • Taipei • New Delhi • Cape Town • Madrid • Mexico City • Amsterdam • Munich • Paris • Milan

PEARSON EDUCATION LIMITED

Edinburgh Gate
Harlow CM20 2JE
Tel: +44 (0)1279 623623
Fax: +44 (0)1279 431059
Website: www.pearsoned.co.uk

First published in Great Britain in 2007

© Pearson Education Limited 2007

The right of Carmel McConnell to be identified as author of this work has been asserted by her in accordance with the Copyright, Designs and Patents Act 1988.

ISBN: 978-0-273-71178-0

British Library Cataloguing-in-Publication Data
A catalogue record for this book is available from the British Library.

All rights reserved. No part of this publication may be reproduced, stored in a retrieval system, or transmitted in any form or by any means, electronic, mechanical, photocopying, recording, or otherwise, without either the prior written permission of the Publishers or a licence permitting restricted copying in the United Kingdom issued by the Copyright Licensing Agency Ltd, Saffron House, 6–10 Kirby Street, London EC1N 8TS. This book may not be lent, resold, hired out or otherwise disposed of by way of trade in any form of binding or cover other than that in which it is published, without the prior consent of the Publishers.

10 9 8 7 6 5 4 3 2 1
11 10 09 08 07

Designed by designdeluxe
Cartoon illustrations by Bill Piggins and Randy Glasbergen

Typeset in 10/15pt IowanOldStyleBT by 30
Printed and bound in Great Britain by Ashford Colour Press Ltd., Gosport

The Publisher's policy is to use paper manufactured from sustainable forests.

CONTENTS

INTRODUCTION

DECIDE TO BE HAPPIER (THE ABC APPROACH)

18 By the way, you're gorgeous

UNDERSTAND
HAPPINESS

CREATE A PERSONAL HAPPINESS PLAN

UNLEARN
UNHAPPINESS

OUR PLAN:
MAKE OTHERS
HAPPY

SOME HAPPINESS PLAN EXAMPLES

PUT YOUR PLAN INTO ACTION

ABOUT THE AUTHOR

CARMEL McCONNELL M.MBA, F.RSA Founder, Magic Breakfast

Carmel McConnell is a social entrepreneur and author. Her background is unusual in combining social activism and senior corporate experience.

In 2001 she founded children's charity Magic Breakfast, (www.magicbreakfast.com). Magic Breakfast delivers free, healthy breakfast food and nutrition education to primary schools in greatest need - feeding 1,000 children each morning. It won the *Guardian* Charity of the Year award in 2005.

To part fund the Magic Breakfast, Carmel founded a social enterprise, Magic Outcomes (www.magicoutcomes.com). Magic Outcomes offers professional leadership training and team development, based in a primary school, with all profits to Magic Breakfast. Magic Outcomes now runs programmes to help low income schools develop social enterprise skills, and create more happiness for everyone in the school environment.

In 2005, Magic Outcomes won the Caroline Walker Trust Social Enterprise Award.

Carmel is a Board member of the School Food Trust, Board member of Social Enterprise London and Fellow of the Royal Society of the Arts.

PUBLISHER'S ACKNOWLEDGEMENTS

We are grateful to the following for permission to reproduce copyright material:

Happiness Diagram from Layard, R., *Happiness*, Penguin Books, 2005, © Richard Laynard, 2005; Excerpt from Cameron, D., 'Danes The Happiest People in Europe: Survey', April 17, 2007, Copyright 2007 Reuters. Reprinted with permission from Reuters. Reuters content is the intellectual property of Reuters or its third party content providers. Any copying, republication or redistribution or Reuters content is expressly prohibited without the prior written consent of Reuters. Reuters shall not be liable for any errors or delays in content, or for any actions taken in reliance thereon. Reuters and the Reuters Sphere Logo are registered trademarks of the Reuters group of companies around the world. For additional information about Reuters content and services, please visit Reuters website at www.reuters.com. License # REU-1668-MES; City & Guilds, excerpt from 2007 Happiness Index. The original author and copyright holder of this information is City & Guilds. No information can or should be reproduced without written consent from City & Guilds. (www.cityandguilds.com); A Spoonful Of Sugar from Walt Disney's MARY POPPINS, Words and Music by Richard M. Sherman and Robert B. Sherman © 1963 Wonderland Music Company, Inc., Copyright Renewed, All Rights Reserved, Used by Permission.

In some instances we have been unable to trace the owners of copyright material and we would appreciate any information that would enable us to do so.

AUTHOR'S ACKNOWLEDGEMENTS

Thank you.

This book has been helped by the kindness of many people. I'd like to thank Richard, Rachael, Laura and Lucy at Pearson Education for their advice and patience!

Thanks also to Elie and Mel at Magic Breakfast, and those who were kind enough to be interviewed, or disclose their own personal happiness plans.

Thank you to Daniel Rosen, Frances Maguire and others who contributed their wisdom along the way.

In particular I'd like to thank Catherine for her love and support while I wrote this. You make me happy.

WHEN AND WHERE ARE YOU HAPPIEST?

Close your eyes, think about it.
Then note whatever comes to mind here.

"I'm happiest when ..."

_____

_____

_____

_____

_____

_____

_____

_____

_____

_____

_____

_____

_____

Or maybe just bear it in mind. I hope to show how to gently encourage more happiness into your life, based on your unique take on it.

Does that sound like a good idea?

Happiness is not achieved by the conscious pursuit of happiness; it is generally the by-product of other activities.

Aldous Huxley

INTRODUCTION

00

Could you be happier?

Is there room for a little bit more happiness in your life? If so, this is the book for you.

It will help you to create a happier life for yourself, if that's what you want. Better still, it will help you towards a happier life *on your terms*, without anyone putting their oar in and telling you what kind of life you should be leading. (I'm guessing that maybe like me, you've had enough of that.)

It's a big subject, so I'm going to focus on *your* happiness. After all, there is no such thing as "one size fits all" when it comes to being happy. This book isn't a rigid ten exact steps that will make every single person happy. It really doesn't work like that. Happy is such a deeply personal thing.

What we need is a flexible, adaptable plan that will gently show you how you can choose to move from where you are now, to a place with more happiness. And that's what you'll find here.

We all know people in life who seem to have it all worked out on the happiness front. Things always seem to go well for them, and even when things do go wrong, they know how to handle it and what to do. What's the difference between them and the rest of us, who find it all a bit of a struggle sometimes?

In my view, there are a few simple basics. Here they are:

1 **Happiness gets created while you're busy doing other things**. It happens when you:

- Set the intention to be happy – whatever you've got to do today
- Live as the "real you"
- Have a choice; for example to know your limits and say no
- Take action
- Put love first

This book will help you get all these things sorted – to help you find the easy way to more happiness. It really doesn't have to be a rare treat; and if that's what you think, I hope to change your mind. Amazingly, taking control of your life in this way is a major step forward when it comes to happiness.

2 **Aiming for happiness as the goal itself is missing the point**. If someone (down the pub, say) told you "my priority right now is to be happier", what would you think? Exactly. It's like saying you are going on holiday to get a tan. Ideally wouldn't it be better to go on holiday to swim in the sea, snorkel, explore, play on the beach, sleep, eat, laugh and visit amazing places? The tan comes along without any effort while you're busy doing all this other stuff. Happiness is exactly the same – if you get your life sorted out generally, and are doing good things that you want to do, then happiness will usually just take care of itself.

3 **More happiness comes from the heart**. Who are you? A messy, unique, gorgeous, imperfect human, that's who. Not a programmable robot, thank God. So, you are more likely

to be happy (for a bit anyway) when you open your heart, rather than strive to follow somebody else's intellectual formula. This book will help you do more on that.

4 **Happiness comes and goes**. It's a fleeting thing, a bit precious. Trying to stay on a happiness high is not a good idea. It's OK to come down. We just want to be a generally happier version of ourselves.

5 **Happiness as an emotional win–win**. It is not possible to think your way to a happier life; happiness is an emotion, a feeling. And it starts, and lasts, from one simple intention; to make yourself happy by making other people happy.

6 **Happiness is not automatic (as we're led to believe)**. The basics of life don't seem to work as well as they ought to. Find a good job, breed and own more than others. It should work, so why doesn't it? Why are we unhappier than ever with so many good things in life? We'll take a look, and hopefully find a way to enjoy our current sources of happiness, as well as create more.

AND IT STARTS, AND LASTS, FROM ONE SIMPLE INTENTION; TO MAKE YOURSELF HAPPY BY MAKING OTHER PEOPLE HAPPY.

7 Happiness is not the answer! It would be great to think there is some secret, an answer to the big questions, some magic wand to wave over our problems. Happiness is being touted in this way, elixir-like, but you know what? In my view, tiny answers come every day, like baby steps, if we're on the right track. And those baby steps take us forward, bit by bit to a happier future, whatever that might look like. I'd love to support you with this.

What this book isn't

I have to quickly and clearly draw a distinct line between what this book aims to do and the growth in "lifestyle gurus". They seem to be everywhere – books, TV, radio. Telling us all what to do and how – what to wear, what to eat, where to live, what to do, how much exercise to take, what to spend, and on and on. Whether it's what we do as individuals or what we do as a society, there's no shortage of experts telling us how to live our lives, in order to achieve their version of "the successful contemporary human being". Their way is the right way and we should all follow it. These experts seem less gurus and more lifestyle fascists to me.

I know this could be a let-down if you were looking for a generic A to Z of happiness, but in my view, there is no one single way to be happy. There are new perspectives to think about and apply to your unique circumstances. There are tips and ideas and some practical suggestions, which I believe can open up new possibilities for a happier life. However, the only way that will help you is *your* way (don't worry, we'll help you find it). So, I won't presume to tell you how to live your life.

Neither is this book a philosophical look at the nature of happiness that explores in great detail why we aren't all as happy as our grandparents. Nor is it an in-depth look at why buying more stuff doesn't make us happy (it doesn't – there, that's covered). There's not a lot of pontificating here. Just lots of personal, purposeful suggestions that have the capacity, if combined with your will, to make you happier. Does that sound OK?

What this book is

I've spent a lot of my life helping people discover:

- How to find purpose and success
- How to build better relationships (at work as well as at home)
- How to take action, outside their comfort zone, in line with their values
- How to create the right level of wealth to live a happy life.

These ideas have helped me to grow less frightened in the face of the scariest bits of scary old life. And the ideas have worked well for thousands of other people too.

The Happiness Plan is a powerful action plan that, if you put your faith and effort into it, will help you make changes.

This book is for you if:

- You think certain parts of your life aren't working
- You just don't have the fire in your belly or joy in your soul that you'd like to have
- You want to make some changes, but aren't sure how.

How will this work?

The Happiness Plan is a way to design your life so it feels happier, more connected, more purposeful.

It has seven steps:

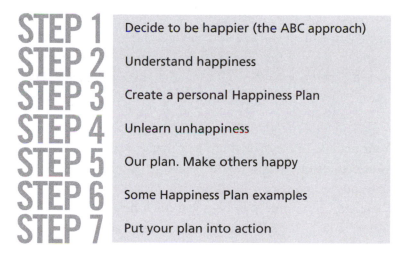

STEP 1	Decide to be happier (the ABC approach)
STEP 2	Understand happiness
STEP 3	Create a personal Happiness Plan
STEP 4	Unlearn unhappiness
STEP 5	Our plan. Make others happy
STEP 6	Some Happiness Plan examples
STEP 7	Put your plan into action

Each one of those steps will have some easy wins, ways to find more happiness here and now. Plus guidance from the experts and exercises for you to gain a better perspective on what is happening right now in your life.

Looking at those seven steps, you may have noticed Step Five 'make others happy'. Why, you might reasonably ask, should your Happiness Plan be concerned with the happiness of other people?

It's because a Happiness Plan based on your needs alone is not going to be enough. We humans are social creatures, and our happiness is inextricably linked to that of others. Trouble is, we've been increasingly trained to think as individuals, with little sense of the communities around us. Creating a more lasting kind of happiness requires investment in our relationships, in the shared connections and purpose that join our families, workplaces and communities together – or which sometimes cause them to break up.

Each step will encourage you to view things differently. For example to enjoy the happiness that may already be there in your life, perhaps wanting a little more of your company. Then move on to the tactics and techniques that will enable you to create even more.

Your plan is, in context, there to enhance your relationships, your connection to work, your sense of belonging where you live and how you see your life's happiness overall. In each of these stages, my aim is to help you think how life would be if you were really happy. Then take the steps to get there.

And this book aims to help you make your mind up to be happier!

> **Most people are about as happy as they make their minds up to be.** Abraham Lincoln

What is a plan?

The Happiness Plan is an approach designed to help you build a happier life. A plan is a statement of intention, a high-level design plus a detailed list of what needs to be done to reach the desired outcome.

This book aims to help you design a happier life for yourself – that's the desired outcome. How will you do that? By asking yourself better questions, opening up to new ideas and, above all, being prepared to try stuff out. The process of learning how to be happier isn't a project with an end date. Instead try to consider happiness as the underlying intention, there to support the many choices and changes in life.

There is no duty we so underrate as the duty of being happy.

Robert Louis Stevenson

DECIDE TO BE HAPPIER (THE ABC APPROACH)

01

The Happiness Plan steps

STEP 1	**Decide to be happier (the ABC approach)**
STEP 2	Understand happiness
STEP 3	Create a personal Happiness Plan
STEP 4	Unlearn unhappiness
STEP 5	Our plan. Make others happy
STEP 6	Some Happiness Plan examples
STEP 7	Put your plan into action

Your life could be an on-going cycle of change for the better. With you setting the pace, deciding the content, trying out the benefits. My suggestion is, becoming happier is not as hard as you think, it doesn't have to be deferred until you retire, or get rich. It doesn't only happen in certain limited situations. Happiness can be as accessible and as everyday as the air we breathe. Does that seem possible to you? Does it seem like the beginning of a Happiness Plan? I hope so.

One of the most powerful ways to get perspective on where you are now is to ask yourself some questions. In its simplest form, the Happiness Plan consists of just three. It could, if you like, be as easy as ABC!

Could I...

A   Allow more room for happiness in my life. Expect it?

B   Begin. What could I do, here and now?

C   Continue the process; it makes me happy!

And yes, that does look very simple. But knowing it and doing it are some distance apart. As anyone who has repeatedly failed to use the life-changing gym membership can tell you. Me? Yes. But I was there in spirit if not in person. And my spirit is now toned, svelte and fit. Just the body to go then. Knowing about it and doing it are very different.

Each of these three questions will have a lot more going on at detailed level – which we'll explore in the coming chapters. For

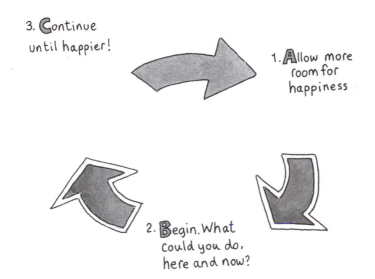

3. Continue until happier!

1. Allow more room for happiness

2. Begin. What could you do, here and now?

The ABC of Happiness Planning

example, the question "Could I allow more room for happiness in my life?" might mean you close your eyes and get the first three thoughts on to the nearest bit of paper. Equally, it might mean learning from psychologists who have been working on trends in individual well-being. Or you might want to ask the people around you, to find out their view of what you could do to be happier, based on your current routines. Each question is a distinct step, which I hope will be both instructive and productive. Instructive because you use a gentle questioning process to learn more about yourself. Productive because you'll be encouraged (and in particular be encouraging yourself) to take action. Trying stuff is the real deal with the Happiness Plan – it isn't just a theory!

There are some lessons that can be applied to anyone, anywhere. And these will always be useful to you if you learn how to use them to ask questions of yourself. Personal change begins with a question, something that has the power to open eyes, to engage your mind. And if the questioning process goes well, I hope you will quickly start to feel some benefits at a personal level.

By choosing to create a Happiness Plan, you'll feel able to

- Create a sense of optimism about the future
- Believe there is a kinder road to success
- Grow your sense of trust in others
- Feel better in yourself, to become your own best friend
- Be better prepared to handle the worst pressure points in life (no money, for example)
- Express "the real you" and discover what you want to do with your life

■ Feel more able to appreciate what you've already got, without the help of your credit card for that urgent next purchase.

You'll be encouraged to look at your life through the lens of happiness. One simple way is consider how happy you are in the major areas of your life – to get a gut feel.

What is most important to you? Creating a happier life means learning more about yourself, which has got to be a good thing. So, take a look at the table below and add however many more "Important area of my life" entries as you need. Then put a tick next to one of the three suggested responses.

Exercise How happy do I feel right now, in each important area of my life?

Important area of my life	I'm happy	I'm unhappy	In between or don't know
Family			
Friends			
Work			
Health			
Finance			
Add next here			

What other areas would you add? And which column would you tick on each? Don't take too long on this – gut feel is what we're after.

How does that look? Write your reaction down here.

I hope you have a few ticks in the first column – but whatever you answered, the Happiness Plan will help you make things better. Starting with something you may not consider very often.

By the way, you're gorgeous

I mentioned gorgeous. That's right, gorgeous. You. But maybe that's not how you feel about yourself?

No one alive has your unique combination of skills, knowledge, dreams. No one feels the way you do, looks like you, has the same relationship with your family. No one loves your friends the way you do. As far as we know, no one has ever been you before, so it follows that no one has tried to do what you are doing.

And the astonishing thing is, although you are unique, a one-off, you do share something with every other person alive. Inside you lies the potential for anything; to achieve beyond your current limits, to do something wonderful, on a small or big scale. You have the potential for so much, your heart holds love and warmth that could light up the coldest evening. You are simply packed with potential.

And yet, at work, and often in our relationships, no one seems to mention this. The yearly appraisal usually says something along the lines of "well done, but try harder next year". Few friends have the inclination to tell you how great you are, even if they sort of know it. So let me tell you again. You are gorgeous, unique and full of potential. You are.

Now, I've a question. How easy has this page been to read? Have you put the book down to puff up a proud breast in recognition of your gorgeousness? Or found it so bad that words can't begin to describe your distaste?

Your reaction – somewhere in the middle maybe – is a good indication of how you see yourself. If you can't bear to be told how gorgeous you are, it might be that you don't believe it. If you read it and smile, you might allow the possibility. This is important, because how you see yourself is linked to how much happiness you feel able to create for yourself. So this is a sort of ready reckoner to start with. So, please could you be brave and go back to the top of this page. And read again.

Right, second time around – what did you feel? Tick which one is nearest your view

"I can see that I am unique, gorgeous and full of potential…"

1. most of the time

2. some of the time

3. never.

This might feel like a rather big jump into some rather personal questions – I hope that is OK. The reason is this. We easily become anaesthetised to our emotional needs, numbed by the effect of daily demands. We don't question the basics very often, perhaps because we fear the answers. If you can use this book to ask questions of yourself, to ask how you really are, you may be pleasantly surprised.

HOW HAPPY DO YOU FEEL RIGHT NOW?

Happiness depends upon ourselves.

Aristotle

UNDERSTAND
HAPPINESS

02

The Happiness Plan steps

STEP 1	Decide to be happier (the ABC approach)
STEP 2	**Understand happiness**
STEP 3	Create a personal Happiness Plan
STEP 4	Unlearn unhappiness
STEP 5	Our plan. Make others happy
STEP 6	Some Happiness Plan examples
STEP 7	Put your plan into action

I have a friend who regularly goes to a fairly modest restaurant in London. The menu never changes, and most customers have no need to see it before they order. In fact, my friend says "if you don't know the menu by now, God love you." Maybe the definition of happiness feels a bit the same – if you don't know what happiness is by now, God love you.

Well, let's assume that life is reasonably happy for you but that it could be better. And you'd like to know more about how that could work.

Starting perhaps, with some definition.

Happiness is the name given to a wide range of positive emotions, ranging from a quiet satisfaction to euphoric joy and elation. The opposite, say misery or sadness, can range from a sense of mild disappointment to the illness of clinical depression.

Sometimes the normal emotions of sadness are essential to wellness – feeling a deep well of sorrow when grieving is healthy; locking up feelings to "put on a brave face" isn't. Misery is part of being alive, and as joined to happiness as night is to day, or a low to high tide. Happiness and unhappiness are normal emotions on the spectrum of feeling. Sometimes, though, it seems as if misery is forbidden, or that feelings of sorrow or grief are somehow to be minimised, put away quickly. The Happiness Plan includes a warm welcome for your unhappy self, strange as that might sound, because those emotions have as much place in a healthy and balanced life as happiness.

What is to be avoided, however, is the practice of staying in neutral. By this I mean the practice of locking your emotions into an icebox of daily denial and restraint. This effort of emotional suspension can keep your feelings out of the public eye – perhaps even out of your own view.

Staying in neutral might mean, for example, pushing away a family problem day after day, in order to focus on a particularly demanding work project. Or it could mean emotional denial about a health problem, just in case it is something you can't cope with. Life in emotional neutral is usually the result of fear or exhaustion, and although perhaps easier in the short term, it causes all sorts of problems, if not immediately then down the line.

The first step – to allow room for happiness – will help here. If your life is super-packed with busyness, or you cart around the family worries like a 1950s' rucksack, where is the room for your emotions? See your own, unique form of pleasure, or social connection, or purpose, and aim for it. Even if you don't always get there, you'll be aware of the need.

So the Happiness Plan advice is to make room to feel whatever feelings are there to be felt, at the moment you feel them. You can't put your heart on hold for long without serious repercussions. So go ahead, feel the feeling and feel it anyway (with a large nod of respect to Dr Susan Jeffers!).[1]

THE HAPPINESS PLAN ADVICE IS TO MAKE ROOM TO FEEL WHATEVER FEELINGS ARE THERE TO BE FELT, AT THE MOMENT YOU FEEL THEM.

We'll look at this idea of emotional neutrality in more detail later – it isn't always easy to know if you have become acclimatised to a life with less emotional activity because the demands of your life cause you to ignore your needs. Or if you are simply not like that! Clearly no one should be asked to emote outside their personal comfort zone. Unless they guest on daytime chat shows...

Going back to the definitions, happiness is a spectrum of feeling, and at any one time you and I could be, well, anywhere on that spectrum.

[1] *Feel the Fear and Do it Anyway* by Dr Susan Jeffers (Arrow Books, 1991) is a really good book on this subject.

You might want to consider this question held up to the major strands of your life.

In your work right now – where are you?

At home?

Your health and well-being?

With your family?

With your closest friends?

Just gut feel – does that seem to add up to an overall positive? Or a negative? Perhaps the table we saw earlier might help.

Important area of my life	I'm happy	I'm unhappy	In between Or don't know
Family			
Friends			
Work			
Health			
Finance			
Add next here			

At the unhappy end of the spectrum, we experience negative emotions such as sadness, depression, feelings of gloom and despondency. These have physical attributes – tears of grief, the sense of nervous agitation when lost, the pained facial expressions and body language of someone who is engulfed in sorrow.

And at the other, happy end of the spectrum, we experience positive emotions such as joy, pleasure, joviality, perhaps even bliss. And these also have physical attributes – tears of joy, the desire to hug and kiss loved ones at moments of great delight, and the smiles and laughter of pleasure.

Furthermore, it seems happiness has two dimensions (as shown on the diagram on the next page). Psychologists call these two forms "aroused or unaroused" happiness. Aroused, by their definition, is energised, animated. Unaroused is more passive, damped down.

The more energised and animated kind of happiness is joy, a feeling which is more likely to be expressive and physical. Joy – the moments after a call confirming your (wonderful) exam results, for example. The less energised form of happiness is contentment, something which is more likely to be felt within, not necessarily expressed outwardly. Contentment, perhaps the quiet, easy satisfaction you feel when the garden finally looks like one, rather than the wilderness project you moved into. Or when your boss has been averted from another nerve-crunching customer mishap, thanks to a few quiet words on the way over.

On the unhappy end of the spectrum we can see that the more energised and animated kind of misery is agitation, once again something more likely to be expressive and physical. Agitation could be the twenty minutes you spend en route to the airport, when the train decides enough is enough and stays put an hour before your flight. The less energised form is depression.

Depression can range from a touch of "the blues" when life turns temporarily gloomy, right the way to a serious illness which requires expert therapeutic and medical support, medication and lots of recovery time.

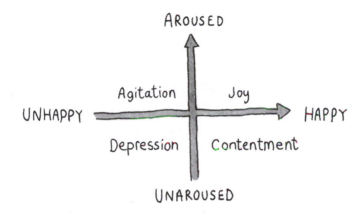

Source: Happiness by Richard Layard (2005)

Obviously each one of these four expressions varies in intensity, but it seems helpful to have a map in any case. To finish the definitions, here are a couple more interpretations of happiness:

> By happiness I mean feeling good – enjoying life and wanting the feeling to be maintained. By unhappiness I mean feeling bad and wishing things were different.
> Richard Layard (2005)[2]

[2] Richard Layard (LSE Economics Professor and Government adviser on happiness). See his Happiness: Lessons from a New Science (Allen Lane, 2005).

Martin Seligman – seen as the founder of positive psychology – identified three distinct levels of happiness:

1 **The Pleasant Life:** Satisfying the visceral pleasures of the body such as having a glass of good wine, a hot bath or a walk in the park. Such pleasures are transitory and superficial and cannot produce true well-being but can make life enjoyable for a moment.

2 **The Good Life:** Engaging in activity, often social in nature, which causes vigorous enjoyment through a challenge – for example, taking up Sunday football or writing a book.

3 **The Meaningful Life:** The highest level of sustained happiness comes when people can give a wider meaning to their lives. Helping others through politics, voluntary work or religion can help people to realise that there is something bigger and more important than themselves.

Martin Seligman (2003)[3]

Happy: Lucky, fortunate, contented with one's lot. Glad or pleased. Felicitous.
The Oxford English Dictionary

[3] Martin Seligman, *Authentic Happiness* (Nicholas Brearley, 2003).

Finally, something I found through my very own detailed research:

> **"Happi"; A loose Japanese coat.**
> *The Oxford English Dictionary*

Yeah, OK.

The best definition of happiness is *your* definition, sown in your own heart, grown in the comfort of your own lifetime. This is something I feel strongly and will argue throughout the book. The idea of buying or installing an off-the-shelf "programme of happiness" feels pretty false – as does the idea that happiness can be pushed like a product through pills or miracle programmes. The Happiness Plan will work best if it is yours, and grows organically. As Voltaire said, "We must each cultivate our own garden".

I hope that gives you enough definition for now, and we've more than covered arousal as far as I'm concerned, thank you very much. Next, let's deal with any doubts about this whole Happiness Plan idea.

Is there room for cynicism?

Of course. There has to be – about this and any other advice on how to improve your life. That's healthy.

As we discussed earlier, happiness grows from a well-lived life, defined as one that is full of your unique sources of happiness. It could be your children perhaps. Or your amazing talent with a team. Feeling well enough to go back to work after an illness, maybe?

The Happiness Plan keeps the question "What can *I* do to be happier?" at the top of your list of things to do, as well as the question "What can *we* do to be happier?" The Happiness Plan is a practical device to pull your values, your unique talents and loves, like a thread through the chaos and wonder of being human and alive. It joins the dots of random events so that what is most important to you continues to shine through, no matter how much pressure you have to handle, no matter how many diverse demands intrude into your day. It is a promise you make to yourself, to stay in touch with what's most important to you. Knowing that you can tap into your sources of happiness is a valuable inner resource to possess. Knowing who you are, and what matters to you, is an essential first step. That, linked to the most exciting new insight into what makes us happy will create a truly powerful combination. It is possible to build a happier life, consciously, openly. There are no impossible pre-conditions for happiness and the voluminous

What's Your Happiness Plan?

Never stop mentally or physically (as long as my brain and body will let me), spend as much time as possible with those who are loved ones and dear friends, and never stop "giving".

Kris Engle, founder of the Bagel Factory Ltd

research seems to suggest that each individual can improve their store of joy with a little thought and direction.

But that said, the question of chasing happiness is, as C.P. Snow mentioned, a highly suspect occupation!

> **The pursuit of happiness is a most ridiculous phrase; if you pursue happiness you'll never find it.** C. P. Snow

Happiness appears as a series of moments occurring spontaneously, so a book offering a foolproof Happiness Plan is like someone offering a no-miss plan to see a dolphin leap skyward from a Cornish sea, or foretelling exactly when you get the first kiss. Can't do it. So, sorry, this is not going to be a "how to, simple guide" full of honest but, in my view, over-optimistic advice.

And one more thing. Sadly, or gladly, there is no generic way to guarantee your personal happiness. As individuals we are too gorgeously bespoke, unplanned and free to do that. There are simple steps that we can take to increase the likelihood, but no more than that.

However, if we encounter the odd guru with a decent-looking happiness formula, let's be open minded. You never know.

Now, what would you like to do next? We've two choices. First, we can try to understand some of the startling new evidence about our happiness, to make sure you've got all the background. Or we could make a start on your bespoke plan. A bit more background? OK. Let's do that.

WHAT DO THE EXPERTS SAY ABOUT HAPPINESS?

What do the experts tell us?

As we settle into this new century, it seems a better understanding of what makes us happy has become a Holy Grail subject. With happiness (in the UK at least) now at lower levels than in the 1950s, the question is being asked – why isn't our affluence making us happy? There are a few theories. One says that we have lost our human connectedness to institutions that used to matter more. In developed countries, we may have distanced ourselves from the rituals of faith, and we seem to have lost our faith in politicians and the certainty of work. Some could say that work takes up more and more space, as does, quite neatly, spending the money we work so hard for. Why is it that the richest countries are also those with the highest rates of depression, where more people claim to be unhappy than happy? We seem to be a less than happy lot, caught up in a financially-driven rush, losing sight of the more important things in life – our close relationships for example – while we urgently make money to spend on the material goods we believe we need.

Why is this?

The science of happiness has grown from that question, and the whole new area of positive psychology. Would it be worth a quick understanding of how this new science of happiness came to pass? OK.

The psychology profession developed in size and became a growth industry in the US just after the Second World War. Veterans came home traumatised, requiring urgent medical attention to their minds as well as bodies. Psychiatrists were a scarce and expensive resource; so clinical psychologists adapted their expertise to offer a less intensive form of support for the homecoming troops. This is one major reason why psychology has been the study of mental illness, with much less focus on good mental health.

However, a major shift has occurred during the past ten years, much of it down to one person. Psychologist Martin E.P. Seligman and his colleagues have successfully turned that post-war focus away from the negative – mental illness – towards the positive, by studying optimism, signature strengths, virtue and well-being. This work has invented a new science, that of positive psychology, which promotes happiness and well-being, not just the study of illness. Seligman's books include *Learned Optimism* (1991) and *Authentic Happiness* (2003), strongly recommended if you want a more detailed view of how this change has come about.

Since Seligman, the numbers people have turned their hand to "happiness economics", adding a measure of "subjective well-being" or SWB to the existing financial measures of economic growth.[4] In the UK, happiness has become a political football, with politicians wanting to examine how happy people are, and turn that into policy or law or what we teach children. Many have written about how the way to happiness isn't via money or possessions (the anti-consumer lobby).

For my part, the study of happiness seems to offer a shortcut, at personal, local and national level – a new way to think about how we can live more connected lives. By connected I mean

[4] Richard Layard, *Happiness: Lessons from a New Science* (Allen Lane, 2005).

that we are more aware of our emotional and social needs, more able to trust and feel a sense of shared purpose with those around us. The positive psychology movement has generated great energy and has opened up a new level of debate about how we can evolve as humans. In the UK we now hear about happiness tsars, happiness lessons in schools and happiness programmes on TV. Perhaps we can develop happiness as a social compass, as much as a personal one, to help us build a less divided society. Can you imagine how good that might be? Anyway, enough of my outpourings of optimism...

To consider next – what has this exciting new science of happiness brought to light? Given the recent profusion of research and book titles on the subject, you might be forgiven for feeling a bit overwhelmed. I've tried to summarise some of the most significant new areas of knowledge about happiness – although this is subjective of course. I've prioritised three areas:

- Happiness and health
- Happiness through income and possession
- Happiness as a national attribute.

Happiness improves health

How you feel most of the time – your habitual emotional state – is a good way to predict how healthy you will be. It seems that anxiety, unhappiness and depression increase the stress hormones, which over time build up health problems by placing the body on a full-time state of high alert. In physical terms, this means that blood is pumped to muscles, and sugar and adrenalin are called into action. This is fine in short bursts, but living in a state of high alert takes more energy, diverts away from non-urgent body functions, and is generally a bad idea, health-wise.

On the positive side, the most famous research on the link between a long life and general cheerfulness concerns a group of nuns (the American School Sisters of Notre Dame) in 1932. Nuns are thought to be a good study group because they lead fairly stable lives in an enclosed community. Well, these nuns were asked by their Mother Superior to keep a diary and to each write a short autobiography. The writings of each nun have shown something quite startling. Those who wrote of positive emotions tended to live longer than those who wrote their autobiographical sketches with more negative emotions. In fact, the nuns who described their "happy previous year" or "looking forward with eager joy" were more likely to live to a ripe old age than those who did not. Ninety per cent of the nuns who were judged to have the most positive emotion were still alive at the age of 85. By contrast, amongst the group of nuns who were the least positive, only 34 per cent were still around at the age of 85. Same diet, similar routines, locations, challenges. One key differentiator: a positive outlook.

It's not how much *you've* got, it's how much *they've* got!

Here is proof that keeping up with the Joneses has some mileage after all! It seems that material gains and losses are felt most acutely in relation to other people. In one study, students at Harvard were asked if they'd prefer a low income, knowing their peers were on about the same amount. Or if they'd prefer a much higher income, in the knowledge that their peers earned even more. The majority of students chose lower pay and peer parity. That seems to make no logical sense, does it? So what is going on?

One reason is that levels of happiness through income and any kind of material possession are relative to our perception of what others own. The happiness a manager might feel with a brand new laptop (the only one in the department in fact) is severely curtailed when a box of 20 arrive for the whole office. Our status and hierarchy needs seem to outweigh the actual pleasure of ownership.

Trust in a society predicts happiness levels

Countries where larger numbers of people agree that "generally, people are to be trusted" also score highest on subjective well-being (SWB).

DANES ARE THE HAPPIEST PEOPLE IN EUROPE

Scandinavians may spend a lot of the winter in darkness but they are the happiest people in Europe, according to a study released this month.

Countries like Denmark and Finland scored highest on the study of happiness in Europe carried out by Cambridge University, which also found that the sunny southern countries of Italy, Portugal and Greece got the least joy out of life.

The survey entitled: "No Man is an Island" revealed that countries where people enjoy time with friends and family, have

Source: "Danes the happiest people in Europe: survey" reported by Reuters Press, April 2007

trust in government and national institutions were more likely to be happy than those living in a sunny climate.

The study rated respondents on their overall sense of happiness and life satisfaction on a scale of 1 to 10.

Danes – who expressed a high level of trust in their politicians and public institutions – came top of the field at 8.3. Italians – who reported lower levels of satisfaction with their national quality of government – came last at 6.49.

"Italy, Greece, Portugal, Germany and France report the lowest levels of happiness whereas the Scandinavian Countries, Netherlands and Luxembourg report the highest," the study said.

Although Europeans are generally four times wealthier than their fathers and grandfathers, their levels of happiness are either equal to or lower than 40 years ago.

THE LITTLE THINGS THAT SAY A LOT ABOUT YOUR EXPECTATION OF HAPPINESS

I know this is neither possible nor desirable, but if I was to stand next to you, right now, and ask "How are you?", what would you say? Tick one:

"Really good thanks"
"Not too bad...."
"I've been better..."
"OK, I suppose, considering..."

"Fine thanks, how are you?"

"Mustn't grumble…"

"In the pink"

"Fabulous darling"

"How did you get in?"

What is your normal, everyday answer to the question "How are you?" If not one of the above, jot it down here:

_____

_____

_____

_____

Is that how you are? What if you upped the fabulousness for a day? Took whatever your normal response would be and turned it up, just a notch, to something that described you, only happier. Try it. Go on.

Major influences on your happiness

How happy are you right now? If you are feeling pretty good, do you know why?

Quiz Influences on happiness

Which of the following do you think most likely to influence your happiness, day to day? Put a tick (mental or otherwise) next to the following:

1 Winning a million on the lottery

2 Being globally mobile – able to live anywhere in the world

3 Becoming severely disabled following an accident

4 Losing your home through bankruptcy

5 Having a high genetic happiness predisposition (i.e. happy parents)

6 Having a gorgeous and desirable partner

Which one did you rate highest?

But do you know what? Happiness is only marginally affected by any number of external factors, such as those shown above. Having parents with a predisposition to happiness is more important, according to the research and the science. Half of our total capacity for happiness comes free, with the DNA. That's right. The happiness research shows that number five above – the genetic mix you inherit from your family – makes the biggest difference. In one study[5], identical twins – genetic clones remember – were found to have the same measures of happiness, even when raised separately. Even when their lives followed radically different paths.

[5] Tellegan, A., Lykken, D.T., Bouchard, T.J., Wilcox, K.J., Segal, N.L., Rich, S. (1988) 'Personality similarity in twins reared apart and together', *Journal of Personality and Social Pyschology* 54 (6): 1031–1039.

Seligman calls this genetic inheritance a "steersman" which guides each one of us towards a certain level of happiness. So how cheerful are/were your genes?

Well, on a totally unscientific basis, my happy gene score is 10 cheery genes, 1 dreary gene, based on my parents' demeanour. Clearly not a highly scientific approach, but maybe something to think about.

Did you sit in gloomy rooms listening to gloomy tunes growing up? Or were your bedroom curtains opened each morning by a cheery soul who loved rock 'n' roll and made you laugh? What was it like for you?

Can you recall some event or time with your parents which bears out your score? Have a good think – if 50 per cent of your happiness is drawn from this, perhaps it's worth some reflection. Who else could you ask? What would other members of your family say? How could you measure it?

Just a quick thought for those of us who lost parents at an early age, or who are adopted. The nature vs nurture point is potentially a missing part of the jigsaw. So thankfully there is another 50 per cent to play with. Or am I being an annoying optimist again?

But what about the other items listed in the quiz opposite? Money, mobility, health. They, apparently, make a tiny contribution to subjective assessments of improved happiness, according to a wide range of measures, across all kinds of groups of people.[6] This concept seems astonishing. External

[6] 'Causes and Correlates of Happiness'. In D. Kahneman, E. Diener and N. Schwartz (eds) *Well-being: the Foundations of Hedonic Psychology* (Russell Sage Foundation, 1999).

factors do not make the difference between your levels of happiness or sadness; at most, they add between 8 and 15 per cent to the total variance on individual happiness.

Here is a list of factors that do *not* greatly enhance your long-term happiness:

- Money
- Where you live
- Health
- Faith
- Marital status.

You might find this hard to believe, and it is worth having a look at the reasoning of the first of those (we'll consider the others elsewhere in the book).

Money

When average purchasing power reaches £10k per person (measured by economists as the Gross National Product) the extra income doesn't make a substantial difference to your satisfaction with life. Our increased income in the last forty years has not had a jot of positive impact on our sense of life satisfaction. In fact, a survey carried out for the BBC in 2006 found that only 36 per cent of Britons would describe themselves as "very happy", compared to 52 per cent in 1957.

In his book, *Authentic Happiness*, Martin Seligman had this to say on the subject:

"How important money is to you, more than money itself, influences your happiness. Materialism seems to be counterproductive; at all levels of real income, people who value money more than other goals are less satisfied with their income and with their lives as a whole, although precisely why is a mystery."

So, could this explain some of our malaise? Money isn't going to make us happy unless having more money is a primary goal. I don't know many people like that – and I do know a lot of people who work hard for other goals. To feel professional pride in achievement within their chosen specialism, or who want to make a difference, or who want to create something of beauty.

Many of us work in jobs that have financial incentives, and we are generally encouraged, by advertising, for example, to see a luxury lifestyle as the surest route to lasting joy. But the evidence undermines this. Which means that identifying and concentrating on the true sources of your happiness are even more important than adopting the belief "When I'm rich, of course I'll be happy." Ladies and gentlemen we may have spotted a flaw in the perfect system that causes us to earn and spend in equal amounts each month.

Why more is never enough

Now I'd like to explore this flaw a little more. We're being sold the idea of happiness via more new stuff, but is that really going to work? I'd like to suggest not, and it's because of one big reason.

No amount of purchasing can ever satiate the need for more new stuff. We quickly adjust so the new improved model becomes the old one, to be upgraded. Again, and again, and

Copyright 1996 Randy Glasbergen. www.glasbergen.com

again. Marketing feeds this, of course. But it is worth knowing that the "at last – I'm happy" moment is unlikely to arrive just after you enter your PIN.

Although we expect to feel happier for a long time after we acquire the shiny new whatever, evidence shows that we quickly get used to new material possessions, and they become part of our lives. With each upgrade we adapt, become acclimatised really fast, and the exciting shiny new becomes boring scratched old in nanoseconds. Meanwhile, we remain loyal to our consumerist addictions. I use that word carefully, and it really does apply to the habits of so called "shopaholics". The new item – even the new car or house – doesn't give the lasting sense of happiness that we believed it would. Even though we worked our hearts out for two years to save up for it.

This is partially because of something called hedonic adaptation. The cycle of endless consumerism is known as the

"Hedonic Treadmill". Psychologists describe how we all adapt to positive or negative events and return to our usual levels of happiness – our genetic setting.

To give one example: after many years in a small flat, a young couple upgrade to a new flat with, joy of joys, an extra bedroom. Their very own homely happiness, right? Well yes, briefly. But the longed for, saved for sense of space, peace and individual freedom simply fails to materialise. After a few months in the new home they cannot imagine how they ever survived in one bedroom. Another few laps on the Hedonic (defined as relating to pleasure) Treadmill.

It seems that nothing you can buy will ever make you feel you've got enough. It can make you feel good, fantastic or even like another person, but it can't satisfy your need to replace, upgrade, re-do, improve and get a bigger one. You and I are insatiable. So it's possible that your Happiness Plan could save years and years of working hard, saving to buy stuff, and then finding a way to recycle it twelve months on. Doesn't that dissolve some of the attraction of eternal spending? Until the next time you get pole buying position in front of your favourite things anyway.

Maybe it's time to think about why you work so hard; maybe you need to take some time off instead. Find your inner activist/gambler/sloth or something. Or else work another weekend to buy something you might not even need. Your call.

Linked to this rather scandalous news on Hedonic adaptation is the emphasis on becoming individuals who are more finely aligned to the shops than to anything else. Where all the hard study and scrambling up some career ladder is entirely aimed at making us financially better able to buy new stuff.

In my view, we've over-developed one side of our lives – that of the affluent achiever. Affluent achievers must be happy, mustn't they? Doing well at work, enjoying an expensive lifestyle?

Whoever this person is, they've worked hard and maybe made sacrifices in terms of family and personal time.

How many of us though become trapped in a struggle for more pay and recognition at work while neglecting the simple pleasures that humans need – good quality time with friends and family, or a walk in the park?

Well, if that is the case, the trap is causing problems. Work-related stress has never been higher: stress-related health problems cost the NHS £3 billion each year. A range of social commentators tell us how our communities are woefully disrepaired.

Of course this is a generalisation – there are many fulfilled, healthy, family-balanced success stories at the top of the work tree. Aren't there? Surely boardrooms are full of people who have reached the pinnacle of their careers by equalling the needs

"You said I should spend more time with our children, so I turned their faces into icons."

Copyright 1996 Randy Glasbergen. www.glasbergen.com

of work with the needs of their loved ones, equalling the time spent in meetings with the time spent relaxing? What's that? You don't know any. Funny that – nor do I. The hard-working affluent achiever has brought economic growth, a country with high home ownership and plenty of consumer confidence. But has this financial success brought us more contentment, health or security? I'm not so sure. Certainly the evidence points to less, not more, feelings of satisfaction as a result.

And what about the world outside where you work? In most developed nations, the division between the "haves and have nots" has increased.[7] Many young people view the future with distrust.[8] The elder generation long for a lost sense of community and belonging – the kind that kept the backdoor unlocked and made a nice cake for the village fete. We've become, in my view, somewhat detached from some major sources of happiness, in our drive to increase achievement and financial success.

That's not to say that happiness is divorced from material comfort or financial security; however the emphasis has become skewed. Financial security is surely to enable more time to enjoy the sources of our happiness, whether that is family or flying or philandering. But often the search takes every available hour – and that just can't be right.

Back to this thing about being gorgeous, unique, unprogrammable human beings.

We need to hear the music of the soul, luxuriate in the long lie-in, insist on a kiss in the sunshine. Preferably with someone you know.

---

[7] End Child Poverty Report, *Unequal Choices* (2006), www.endchildpoverty.org.uk/publications/html
[8] Unicef Study into Child Wellbeing (2007).

WE NEED TO HEAR THE MUSIC OF THE SOUL, LUXURIATE IN THE LONG LIE-IN, INSIST ON A KISS IN THE SUNSHINE.

Exercise Try this! A little appreciation of what you've already got

What I've already got – tick one column

	Yes – describe	No
1. Does anyone love me?		
2. Am I solvent (ish)?		
3. Am I able to earn a living?		
4. Are my closest loved ones OK?		
5. Is my health reasonably good?		
6. Do I have hobbies or interests I enjoy?		
7. Am I able to look after my basic needs?		
8. Do I have somewhere to live?		
9. Do I have enough to eat?		
10. Does my work look like it could continue?		

Yes this is very basic – it just seems that we take so many things as normal, essential ingredients in our lives, when their presence is pretty good news. Why do we all stress about getting even more, when we could be doing OK? It's a draining, demanding process, and no one feels it more than the affluent achiever.

I am suggesting that ignoring the need for happiness is starting to look like an outdated model for a new era. The Happiness Plan is a way to make sure that your success is achieved without sacrificing your humanity. Affluence and achievement are not worth fighting for if we lose our sense of appreciation along the way. Appreciation of:

- What's going well in your life
- Easy, loving relationships
- Your marvellous physical attributes (!)
- Your playlist
- Who loves you.

Maybe we're talking about a Happiness Plan that allows the affluent achiever to evolve a better sense of appreciation along the way. How many times do we need to read successful captains of business saying "I sure wish I'd stopped to smell the roses along the way" or "If I had to do it all again, I'd make sure I slept with Mary"? Oh, sorry, that was someone's secret.

Say you fast forward. Imagine that your life, just as it is now, continues pretty much unchanged for the next ten years. Would you look back at the end of that time and say:

"I sure wish I'd appreciated

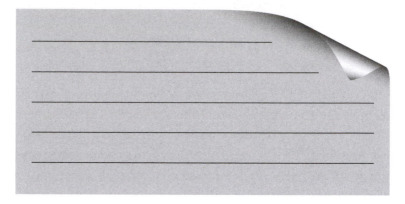

more"

Anything? Perhaps your Happiness Plan can remind you to tune into the things you can appreciate here and now. Each day could be a rich playground, full of things you are looking forward to – and missing out on here and now. Here and now, look around. What big beautiful thing sits in your life? You sure you're too busy to enjoy today?

Evolving to a happier kind of affluence

What about a different kind of affluent achievement – one with an added Happiness Plan ingredient – appreciation?

Success at any price is not really the best idea. Not when it costs your soul, your health and your relationships. And anyway, like I said, it's starting to look outdated. In the new economy, your personal happiness is going to be a key ingredient in the success of your organisation. More and more organisations realise that talented individuals are keen for meaning and purpose within the day job. With time to lead enjoyable lives outside of it.

A happier kind of affluence

Good points if you are in a life chasing affluence and achievement	Bad points	Get the balance – add appreciation. Ask yourself "When and where am I happiest?" for example
Financial security	Debt, dependence on employer/market	How much money do I really need to be happy? What do I enjoy spending money on right now? Do I need to spend so much to enjoy life?
Home ownership	Mortgage trap	What is good about where I live right now? What does my family enjoy about our home? What makes this a home?
Successful career	Stress, loss of work/life balance	What do I love about my work? What gives me that feeling of fulfilment and recognition?
Hedonistic lifestyle	Quest for the next experience or purchase high	What do I enjoy most? Do I notice what I've already got near me, the things I already own?
What are the best parts of your success?	And the bad parts?	And how might you be able to balance with appreciation?

Oh yes. There is a strong argument for the link between creating an attractive organisation and creating happiness – employees who feel motivated by their work may well be more productive. Employees who feel appreciated and recognised often give more in terms of loyalty and goodwill.

When I asked you to write "When and where am I happiest?" did your answer include your line manager? Thought not. Work can offer challenge, fulfilment possibly. It can be where you grow friendships, grow your mind, your skills, your expertise. The workplace is definitely somewhere we can be happy.

But over the years of asking audiences "When and where are you happiest?" only one person ever said "At work". Did I mention that before?

And, when I ask "When and where are you happiest at work?" the answers are in the same top five:

I'm happiest at work when:

1 I feel like my effort makes a difference; that can be for customers, or colleagues
2 My work is recognised in some way
3 We get some challenge sorted out – solving problems
4 I support my team, give them some good leadership to help them grow
5 We all work as a team, everyone included.

By the way – when and where are you happiest at work?

I'm happiest at work when ...

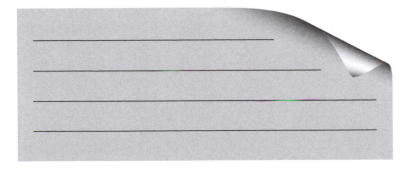

If, even for a split second, you wanted to say 6pm Friday – this is data!

And if you want a quick and easy team build exercise, just get everyone to close their eyes and answer that question. The Board – why not? Your customers – why not? Asking about happiness is a shortcut to find out what really matters to people. And you won't need consultants!

Unfortunately, work also has the potential to create unhappiness. Technology means eternal access, longer hours; we feel the pressures of less job security. I've yet to see an email response with "Sorry, I'll get back to you during my paid working hours".

No wonder we're tired, in need of a drink or a "treat" to relax at the end. No wonder we've little mental or emotional space left for the kids, the neighbours, or anyone apart from the boss. Maybe the core premise of your Happiness Plan is not only a gentle way to increase personal happiness, it could also help to re-prioritise working relationships along more human lines. To take time for our heart, our relationships. Maybe, if this becomes a choice for lots and lots of people, the concept of staying on plan (the Happiness Plan) could become a remedy for some of the social failure we see all around us. It will make our lives better, as well as make a difference.

OK. Big stirring vision for society over.

So what does make a difference to individual levels of happiness, if not the things we all thought (like money, education, occupation or health)? What really makes a difference is YOU.

How to become happier

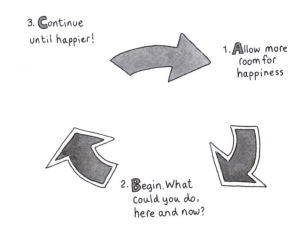

3. Continue until happier!

1. Allow more room for happiness

2. Begin. What could you do, here and now?

Do you want to make certain parts of your life a bit happier? A lot happier perhaps? Then use the ABC approach.

A Allow more room for happiness in that area.

B Begin it – what action do you need to take?

C Continue – until you feel happier.

To allow more room for it, begin something you know makes you happy, and continue. Tactics wise, you might want to set a few short term goals. Stop (no – shoot) me if I get all management on this – but if I gave you a magic wand, said "change three things so you could be happier" what would you say?

One group of friends did this very exercise. They each had three wishes.

They came out with some surprising answers.

- Spend more romantic time with my partner
- Find a part time job which is fulfilling and purposeful
- Sort out some urgent health problems in my family.

That magic wand is in your hand now. What are your three wishes?

If I could change three things so I could be happier, I'd change …

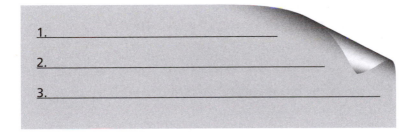

1. _____

2. _____

3. _____

Is it possible that you could do something about this – could you allow more room for any of those?

You know what has to be done. Question is – do you want to enough?

I suppose there might be some problems when you and I choose to simplify something as complex as human happiness. How about we face those together? OK, you may have spotted that I'm not being entirely serious about this. I've read rather a lot of very brilliant research about happiness that seems to add up to the three things in our happiness ABC:

1 Intend to be happy, make some room for it in your crowded life.

2 Do something you know makes you (and others) happy.

3 And then continue, just keep going.

Of course there are going to be obstructions, reasons why you can't choose to be happier at certain times, reasons why you don't believe you should be happy in the first place. However, nothing overcomplicated is required in this Happiness Plan; after all, knowing all the details of the history of psychology isn't necessarily going to put a smile on your face.

A Allow more happiness in your life. Expect it.

B Begin. What could you do, here and now?

C Continue the process; it makes you happy!

This three-step process can work in a variety of settings. If you want to become happier in your work, the ABC will help you. If you want to become happier in your closest and most intimate relationship, the ABC will help you. If you just want to feel your gym membership wasn't a complete waste of money, the ABC will help you. When you get the chance, why not choose the easy way to be happy? To allow more room for it right here and now.

In fact, having gone through this inventory a few times, it's not been possible to find any area where the ABC has failed to have a positive impact. So, let's adopt the ABC of happiness as the second part of your Happiness Plan. If you remember, the first was when you answered the question "When and where am I happiest?"

Now let's consider the ABC in a little more detail.

Step A: Allow more room for happiness in your life. Expect it.

What do you allow into your day? Oh, a lot of work, some travel, some foraging for food in local retail outlets, a few household chores, some relaxation time, with or without others, followed by as much sleep as you can get. Did I miss anything major? Oh yes. What about happiness? Of course each one of those parts of your day could, in themselves, be sources of profound joy, but maybe not. Is it the case that after all the day's demands have been met, there is precious little left for your soul? Let's look at how this works, as demonstrated by the story of the stones and the jar.

THE STORY OF THE STONES AND THE JAR

A Physics teacher brought a large glass jar to school one day and asked her students to identify its contents. Large and small stones, bits of rock, worn glass and sand, they replied. The teacher then asked them to tip the jar over, spilling all the contents, then to refill it carefully, starting with the sand. Each group of pupils tried – and each found that there was never enough room to fit all the stones and large rocks. It seemed impossible.

Finally the teacher instructed them to refill the glass jar, this time starting with the large rocks, and finishing with sand. The rocks fitted in, and the sand simply nestled around the larger stones, until all contents were back inside the large glass jar. The pupils (being like that) asked the teacher about the point of the exercise. Her reply? "When we started with the smaller items, and put those in first, it became impossible to add the larger rocks and stones. There just wasn't room. This is also the case in life. If you fill your lives up with lots of less important things, you won't be able to fit in the bigger, more important things."

Seeing a range of quizzical expressions, the teacher carried on: "OK, here is my take on it. Apart from this being a Physics lesson, I want you all to remember that your life is the glass jar. There are physical constraints on how much you can put into it. So remember to put the most important aspects of your life into each day first, and fit everything else around those."

How does your glass jar look? Back to that day's contents from a moment ago. Full of work, then more work, travel, looking after your survival needs, chores, looking after the kids, some relaxation time, social time – with or without others, followed by sleep. Well, might it be a caring idea to allow more room for happiness in your life? Would you consider a reminder to yourself, say, tomorrow morning? Like a note on your phone about your meetings? Only this time to suggest that your day could also contain more of the things that make you happy, from whichever source and in whichever form. Put your happiness in first; there may not be enough room after the biggest demands of your time, such as work or looking after others, have been prioritised.

In some ways, life would be easier if we got a "life full" message bleeping somewhere to stop the very common problem of taking on more than we have the capacity to do. If each day had some glass, wall-like boundary to show how much could reasonably be put in. But it doesn't, and we end up saying yes to all sorts of things. But perhaps not yes to as much kindness to ourselves, not enough conversations with our families and loved ones, not enough exercise or time listening to music.

So – the first step. Allow more happiness. In each day, consider happiness.

Decide for yourself: "I'm going to make more room in my life for happiness."

SO – THE FIRST STEP. ALLOW MORE HAPPINESS. IN EACH DAY, CONSIDER HAPPINESS.

Exercise Setting the intention

The major strands of my life	Could I make some more room for happiness?	What would I begin with?	Who else gets more happiness from this?
Home			
Work			
Health			
– add the other major strands here…			

Could a busy parent with young children allow more for happiness? Simon, a lawyer, is at work and feeling OK, but the day is a little flat. He has to finish a report, sort out a new client meeting and get home to bathe the children before the babysitter arrives. On his desk he has a picture of his family and the Happiness ABC. He reads Step A: "Could I allow some more happiness in my life today?" What could I make room for?"

A big zero springs to mind. In fact, he remembers the weekend when the family had a brilliant day at the beach – and it seems a million miles away. He carries on. What kind of happiness could I allow? Then he gets an urgent email from one of the partners, and it's back into rush mode again.

What has happened? Well the memory of something wonderful (the family day out) might seem to do more harm than good. He might feel the loss of contact with his family while at work. However the net effect is positive; replaying memories like this will cause his body to experience some physical benefit from remembering – and replaying – the feeling of being in the sun, of drying his children with big soft towels after they've all had a splash about in the sea together. Powerful feel-good chemicals have been released into his brain (serotonin – more on this later) and the next task is undertaken with an enjoyable connection to something enjoyable still rippling through his system.

Well, hang on there author. Isn't this fantasy? Surely a memory is just that – how can it also be physiological? Let me try to summarise.

When we replay an event from memory, our brains reintroduce many of the chemicals that were present at the time of the pleasurable or painful experience. We remember nearly hitting the wall when parking the car – and suddenly become nervous again the next time we get behind the wheel. So, while at his desk, Simon enjoys the memory of the beach and feels warmed again.

That's the first thing. Asking yourself the question "How can I allow and expect more happiness?" will transport you to the nearest moment of happiness that your brain can take you to. You are sending a command "find happiness". Which in itself will produce positive physiological changes in your body. Not bad for a ten-second look at question one. Let's go back to Simon and find out what else happens.

He goes back to the directive "Allow and expect more happiness today" and considers the rest of his day. Expect more happiness. Finish report, drive home, bathe kids. Oh – it's Monday – that programme will be on the radio on the way home. I could listen to that. He does, arrives home in a good mood, having chuckled his way through three traffic jams, two sets of road-works and the fact that the babysitter cancelled, leaving him in sole charge of his own children and their maniacal cousins. Good job you looked at your ABC of happiness, Step A, Simon.

The strength of the first ABC step is that it acts as a reminder to enjoy today. To make room for pleasure, for social connection – for fulfilling, engaging activity as well as the stuff that must be done. Which is a good idea in theory, but not often part of everyday practice. The plan in practice is simply not putting off til tomorrow the enjoyment you could be feeling today. Or are you worried that moments of joy are like savings, to be banked until you retire?

So, back to you, reading this here and now. What do you feel about allowing more happiness into your life? And specifically, what happiness could you allow and expect today? Back to your list – against each major strand of your life – can you add anything more?

You may have a distinctly uneasy response to this. Do you feel you even deserve to be happy here and now? Lots of us don't. To a greater or lesser extent, we've all got reasons why we believe we can't be truly happy right here, right now.

For example, each one of us has a role model, conscious or unconscious, usually drawn from within our family – and that person will have laid down "when happiness is appropriate" as a norm in the family.

Say your dad told you to be brave and never show pain with tears. So you spend years being your dad's brave boy, not showing how you feel, even when your heart is breaking. Maybe not the best option. Your Aunty Ethel wants you to be a financial whiz like her husband, who was never able to get his qualifications. So the family are delighted when you opt for accountancy training, even though it delights you slightly less than sunbathing in sleet. You're being a success, because what is most important to you is to make the family proud.

On top of that comes the social aspiration, to have the stuff other people have, live the life others live, and not miss out. Plus the goals you set yourself – to be richer, healthier, more original, more recognised by the time you are, what, 35, 50, 70?

These influences combine with your own unique ideas and characteristics to become the mental backdrop to your day-to-day choices. You can be happy when Aunty Ethel says "Well done Stuart, you'd have made Uncle Stuart proud." You'll be happy when you stay strong and don't cry when you break your leg, though you can't remember the reason for this is your father's voice. You are the kind of person who would be unhappy with a load of blubbing blokes.

Quiz What kind of person are you?

What special mix decides "you are the kind of person who is happiest when...?" Maybe it's time for a bit of thought on that. Are you the kind of person who is happiest when

(a) The credit card balance is less than £2,000 and the bills are paid?

(b) The team at work agree with your view on the big decisions?

(c) Your car/bonus/golf swing makes grown men weep with envy?

(d) All the children get good degrees at university (oh, they're only 3 and 5 years old at the moment. Ah)?

Which means that if you have a firm "I'm only happy when ..." you could be setting yourself up for disappointment. Your Happiness Plan is going to be a guide to understanding this, as much as a way to make changes. So over to you for more info.

Exercise What has to be in place for you to be happy? ...

What are the pre-conditions? (Perhaps look back at what you wrote under "When and where am I happiest?" for clues)...

"In order for me to be happy, these have to be in place ..."

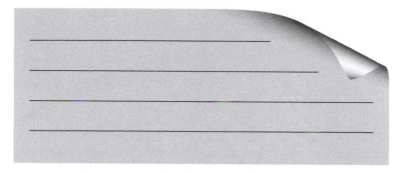

On a scale between 1 and 10 how many of the happiness pre-conditions do you feel are within your control? ...

On a scale between 1 and 10 how much do you think is *out* of your control? ...

How in control of your happiness are you right now? (Again, on a scale between 1 and 10.)

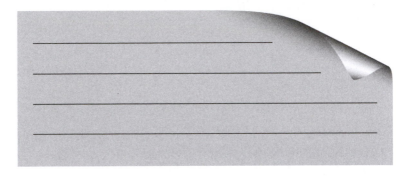

The difference between being happy or unhappy is largely internal. It is driven by our interpretations, expectations.

So the first part of the plan is to map how much of our current Happiness Plan is based on external things (cash, stuff, approval) and how much internal. Then figure out what the right mix for you might look like.

THE DIFFERENCE BETWEEN BEING HAPPY OR UNHAPPY IS LARGELY INTERNAL.

Over the past fifteen years of working with teams and individuals on how to change, I have been struck by how many hold a fixed view of what can happen in their lives. I've heard things like

"I don't expect to\ be happy, now I've got older."

Or

"My personal happiness isn't so important now I've got kids."

And one that really surprised me:

"Of course, my family used to be happy, but the internet put an end to all that."

Excuse me? I never got a chance to ask more.

Maybe you believe you can only be truly happy in certain conditions? Did you pay enough for the holiday to enjoy it properly? Are you sure no one has ever seen this beach before? OK then you can be truly content.

Or at work, what are the strict control conditions under which you can secretly enjoy yourself? None, as work is work and must be endured. OK, fine. Sorry.

I know. Your boss anoints you as the bee's knees. Emails you all the time with special requests. Happy now?

The love of your life decides it's mutual. You cancel the tragedy and get happy/loved up/that duvet day feeling.

What are your pre-conditions about happiness? Do you have a regime that must be followed? If you do, perhaps you are taking the hard road to happiness, the only when really earned and never on Sundays approach. All sorts of smile-filled days could slip by, underenjoyed. We are aiming for a low underenjoyment economy you know.

Whatever you were raised with, please consider going outside your comfort zone to allow more happiness into your life. Don't wait, your heart is open to sunshine at this moment. Love is to be felt, right here and right now – and it is the right thing to do.

Start small. What in your life gives you a warm feeling? Who?

Exercise What do you love about your life?

1 When and where are you happiest? Describe this in as much detail as you can, e.g. what are you doing, where, who is there with you? And yes, you have already answered this question. Don't go back to those answers, just write down the following:

"I'm happiest when…"

2 What enables that to happen? What needs to be in place for you to do this?

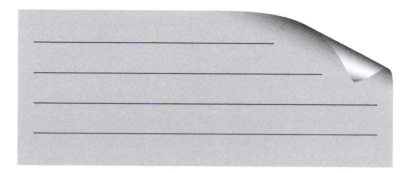

"For me to be really happy, I need to have the following in place..."

3 What else do you love about your life?

■ Who do you love? ...

■ Who loves you? ...

■ What else? ...

4 Do you think others are impacted when you are able to do the things that make you happy? If so, who? And how does it affect them?

"Who knows when I'm happy or unhappy? How does it impact on them? ..."

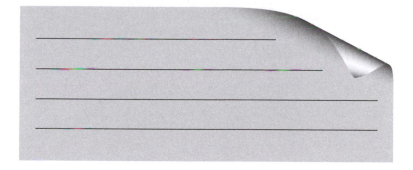

5 What would need to change, so you could do more of what makes you happy?

"The first thing to change, so I could be happier is…"

"Next thing to change..."

"And the next..."

6 Finally, what have you noticed through this process? Anything you weren't expecting?

"I have noticed that..."

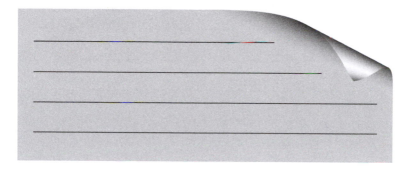

It might take a few goes, this writing about happiness, creating the evidence of what's there. As you ask yourself "When and where am I happiest?" more ideas will hopefully make their way to the surface.

Another way to consider this is to ask the opposite!

Exercise What is most annoying about your life?

1 When and where are you least happy? Describe this in as much detail as you can, e.g. what are you doing, where, who is there with you?

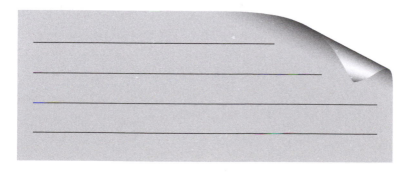

"I'm least happy when…"

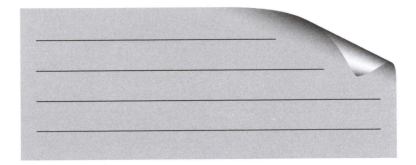

2 What enables that to happen? What needs to be in place for you to do this?

"For me to be really unhappy, the following is usually in place… "

3 What else don't you like in your life?

"Other things I dislike in my life are..."

Sometimes writing the opposite is a bit easier – I don't know if we're naturally critical or just find the good things hide themselves? Anyway, by now, the first bit of evidence is appearing.

What do you think? Is there anything you could choose to do to feel happier today? There is? OK, then what would that be? Is it ...

- Replaying a happy memory
- Talking to someone you care about
- Enjoying the fresh air outside for ten minutes
- Stretching and taking some deep breaths
- Asking for something you need?

Excuse my suggesting a few ideas – I know you'll have loads of your own. Add them here:

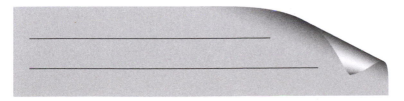

Begin. What could you start with, here and now?

I hope that you found a few ideas to allow some more happiness into your day. Now you just have to get that vital next step – to take action. Here are a couple of suggestions on how.

- Re-read your list, and prioritise, perhaps using a 1 to 10 ranking. Which one do you want most, for example?
- Start small, find something you would like to do without huge demands on your time or effort. The important thing is to try something, be creative about what you could gently adjust in any one day to be a bit happier. Or maybe this is awakening a volcano of change – fine. Start with one small thing. What do you need?

If an image would help, consider these two aspects of your happier life:

1 The changes you'd like to make, to be happier. What did your magic wand exercise bring to light?
2 How hard or easy each change would be to make.

Any plan is secured, held in place by small, winnable targets – the easy wins that build a bit of confidence. Use this table to identify the priorities – the easier to do things, which are actually going to improve your happiness.

And here is an example:

Easy wins

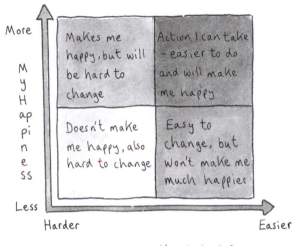

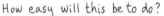

More

M
y
H
ap
pi
n
e
ss

Less

| Makes me happy, but will be hard to change | Action I can take – easier to do and will make me happy |
| Doesn't make me happy, also hard to change | Easy to change, but won't make me much happier |

Harder   Easier

How easy will this be to do?

Easy wins: example - Jon wants more time to
go biking

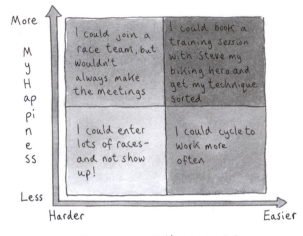

More

My
y
H
ap
pi
n
e
ss

Less

I could join a race team, but wouldn't always make the meetings

I could book a training session with Steve my biking hero and get my technique sorted

I could enter lots of races- and not show up!

I could cycle to work more often

Harder   Easier

How easy will this be to do?

Easy wins: example - you!

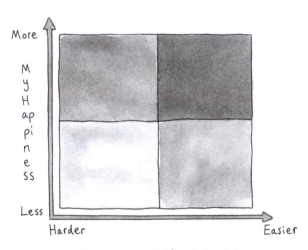

More

My
y
H
ap
pi
n
e
ss

Less

Harder   Easier

How easy will this be to do?

Ten things to stop if you want to be happier

1 Frowning.
2 Leaving the day to other people, e.g. the boss, the loved one or the weatherman.
3 Expecting people to let you down.
4 Saying horrible things to yourself about yourself (e.g. in the mirror first thing).
5 Wondering why others know more cool stuff than you. This is normal.
6 Ignoring other people because you are so busy.
7 Being lazy with the basics (staying up late, eating junk food, staying in all day and all night, never ever doing any exercise).
8 Thinking (a lot) about your biggest regrets and how life is now ruined. Stay in the past and ensure you can't change, why don't you?
9 Asking your best friend for money/favours.
10 Focusing on the things you hate about your job until they make you redundant. In which case, it has been brilliant. Anyone got a tissue?

Start somewhere

What do you most want to change?

How easy or hard will each one of those be to do?

You could go with a gut feel – 1 being easy to change, 3 being hard to change and rank them.

Or just delete those that make your heart sink, and add those that make your heart sing into the appropriate boxes.

OK. What is now in your top right hand corner?

Try it. What do you want to change? Fine. Pick an easy one, and try it.

If you need to give yourself some inner encouragement to get going, try these thoughts. My happiness is important, because I am. (You may hear strong internal disagreement at this point, but press on!) Or, why don't I just trust it'll be OK? And worry less. Trust more, worry less. Was it Woody Allen who said he'd worried sick all his life about things going wrong, and one time it did actually happen? Generally speaking, things do turn out OK. Everything could work out just fine. So enjoy yourself. Cue inner disagreements again!

And now, emboldened with hopes of happiness (!) what about the other factors, circumstances or people who make happiness a win–win for you? Or not. What external factors influence your day-to-day happiness right now?

For each of those, how important is that influence on a scale of 1–10? (1 low, 10 high)

I feel my day-to-day happiness is influenced by the following:

People

_____

_____

_____

Circumstances

_____

_____

_____

Other

_____

_____

_____

> Occasionally in life there are those moments of unutterable fulfilment which cannot be completely explained by those symbols called words. Their meaning can only be articulated by the inaudible language of the heart.
> Martin Luther King Jr.

By now, I hope you are building up a picture of your priorities. Think of these as jottings, playsheets, personal thoughts – the goal here is to explore, not get perfect scores. But the question of who has control over our happiness is pretty interesting.

Continue the process; do more of what makes you happy!

When you start, notice how it makes you feel.

And encouragement really helps. Maybe one conversation in the week with someone you care about, but might not talk to very often. Congratulate yourself on making a small change. Maybe try to get back from work in time to read your child a story. Allow more room for happiness to flood your heart, open your tear ducts maybe. Witness the extraordinary rich detail of your heart.

And the flipside – don't give yourself a hard time if you can't do all you'd like to. This is a plan for your happiness remember!

Over time, build on what you've done and notice what is making you happy. It might be different to your expectations, so try to be open to that and gently stay flexible. Ask yourself questions. Perhaps establish a routine for this like en route to work, or while you brush your teeth. Useful questions might be:

- What do I need?
- What could I do today that would be good fun?
- How am I feeling?
- What would cheer me up today?
- Who could I have a chat to?

Very gently, this could increase your sensitivity to your own needs, and you will become more aware of how you feel and what you need to do. This would be a really big step forward in your happiness planning.

If you put this routine into practice, over time the ABC process will start working its magic. You'll start to notice some changes, including:

- Positive feelings about yourself and your life, as you learn to improve your mental space with more encouragement, less criticism. This will free you up to do more, enjoy more.
- Control, as you understand your day-to-day choices and build a clearer sense of purpose. This could mean gently adapting your current work so you are able to play more to your strengths – in a way that also helps others.
- Greater focus on the sources of your happiness, thereby creating more of a day-to-day sense of well-being, plenty and self-sufficiency.
- A more optimistic, flexible approach to relationships. You may, for example, become more able to see the world through the

eyes of others, and negotiate for everyone's benefit. This is a better strategy than a rigid determination to win at all costs or, at another extreme, playing the eternal victim.

It seems that happy, fulfilled and successful people have decided to choose their happiness, and to plan for it. It doesn't mean they're any less prone to screw-ups, or the blues, or that they have any greater immunity from the worst things that can happen. It just means that they've decided on the happiest life possible, and prioritised aspects of their life to create that.

That was the ABC of Happiness Planning. Allow more room for happiness, begin and then continue. How are you getting on?

It's possible that, having started to listen to your needs, you are ready to take the next step. To help you become even more accomplished at the art of happiness planning. Your *own* happiness.

Happiness is when what you think, what you say, and what you do are in harmony.

Mahatma Gandhi

CREATE A PERSONAL HAPPINESS PLAN

03

The Happiness Plan steps

STEP 1	Decide to be happier (the ABC approach)
STEP 2	Understand happiness
STEP 3	Create a personal Happiness Plan
STEP 4	Unlearn unhappiness
STEP 5	Our plan. Make others happy
STEP 6	Some Happiness Plan examples
STEP 7	Put your plan into action

"My therapy is quite simple: I wag my tail and lick your face until you feel good about yourself again."

Copyright 1997 Randy Glasbergen. www.glasbergen.com

Sources of happiness

Happiness in our lives comes from the sources of happiness. I think we're on a roll here. But it unravels! What on earth are they?

I asked a group of children ranging from 4 to 12 the odd question – what do you get most happiness from in your lives? Answer. From fun. Fun playing sports, fun with friends and fun doing anything really. OK. Now we really are on a roll. So that group of children get happiness from fun. You and I get happiness from – well what?

At national level, we have some clear sources of happiness. We are happy when our freedom is safeguarded, during periods of economic calm. We expect access to good education, to the chance to work and earn our livelihood, to have access to the information we need to run our lives. But are they sources of happiness? In my view, we have to delve into the subjective, personal realm to answer that question. Just as we saw that money only brings happiness if money is an important goal, your sources of happiness are those which line up with your values, your goals and your desires.

On top of that, there are some sources of happiness that seem to do it for everyone. The positive psychologists are specific here.

The quality of our closest relationships comes out first. Then, in no particular order:

- Paid work. For example, unemployment goes hand in hand with depression, loss of self-esteem
- Our social involvement, Wednesday night at bingo, Thursday night in a city boozer (you are busy aren't you?)
- Being married seems to be more of a source of happiness than singledom
- Participation in sport or music
- Voluntary or altruistic activity

It seems to me that, while you could be off to a good and cheery start with a few of these, it is the spirit in which they are lived and enjoyed that matters most. Which brings me to a key part of your plan – being right there and getting a good long heartful of your sources of happiness.

WHAT INFLUENCES YOUR HAPPINESS?

Feel the happiness that's already there

If I could only give you one bit of advice on how to be happier, that would be it.

How can we relax enough to enjoy the pleasures we work so hard for? Or to really be there, heart and mind, when we are physically present? It seems hard to unplug from the stuff we should have done before and need to do for tomorrow to settle down today and have a good one. It seems we just don't savour the here and now, when all kinds of splendid joy could be dancing for us.

The past and future are greedy for our attention. The past wants to replay some memories, or re-wreck ourselves with guilt. The future wants us to fight or dream our way through the theory of tomorrow. Whatever tomorrow holds, it can only get sorted when our physical selves get there. Time enough.

The images of yesterday or tomorrow take over, greedy for our mindshare, taking too much of our time away from this moment. Happiness and sadness happen in our hearts, not our minds. Feelings, emotions belong in the here and now. So if we want to be happier, we need to spend more time in the here and now. Not doing a timelord, ping ponging back and forth through time.

Things to stop worrying about might include:

- The next week at work.
- Getting stressed because next weekend the in-laws are coming and no-one knows what they'll want to do/eat/criticise.

- You haven't phoned your brother for ages because of the row last Easter.
- You don't have a plan for your pension. In particular, what to do when you retire.

Tomorrow's demands are urgent, apparently. Voices say we need to decide what happens when we get there.

Or do we? The pressure of tomorrow's demands can easily make us forget to live today. And today is where the lovely things are, sitting quietly, hoping you'll come back from Planet Plan-it to enjoy the nice afternoon. Being able to notice the nice afternoon? Being able to focus on the sunlight in your front room and how the shadows move across the wall. Blimey.

Don't get me wrong, I'm not knocking patience, endurance and jam tomorrow. I just want to make sure that today gets a look in, jam-wise.

By noticing and being able to enjoy the sources of happiness here and now, perhaps we can create a life with even more

"Jumping from the sofa to the bookcase to the top of the grandfather clock was a lot more fun before they made me wear a helmet!"

Copyright 2003 Randy Glasbergen. www.glasbergen.com

capacity to enjoy tomorrow. What do you think? Maybe it's time to notice the happiness already there in your life.

The first part of your Happiness Plan is to look at what's going on in life just now, with a more appreciative perspective.

Are you on your side?

> The relationship you have with the world is the same as the relationship you have with yourself. Dorothy Rowe

Dorothy Rowe was a psychologist who wrote about the strong human desire to be true to ourselves, to create the fullest possible definition of our lives as a way to well-being. The statement above, from her book *Guide to Life* seems a core concept – suggesting once again that our inner beliefs and values, as well as self-esteem and self-worth, impact most strongly on our happiness in the world.

Assessing your relationship with yourself is not the easiest trick to pull off – perhaps the following three questions will give an idea:

1 Do you believe your promises to yourself (I will leave work at 5, get housework done tonight etc)?
2 Do you like spending time on your own – thinking things through perhaps?
3 Do you feel optimistic, or pessimistic about your future?

Trust your own promises – yes or no?

Time with yourself – a good idea or not?

Good or bad feelings about where your life is headed?

Improved capacity to be happy – in and of yourself – could create closer, warmer relationships with other people. Here is another way to investigate.

Quiz Are you on *your* side?

You go out for an evening with work colleagues, but leave your money at the office by mistake. Do you

(a) Ask someone to lend you enough for the evening, no biggie?

(b) Tell people what has happened and go back to get the money, losing some of the evening?

(c) Call home and ask your beloved to meet you, with cash, at the venue?

(d) Vanish, get a bus home and plan to tell everyone you came over all fluey?

In town one Saturday morning, you park at a meter, forget to put money in, go shopping and return to find a parking fine notice. Do you

(a) Take a deep breath and shout "How could you be so bloody stupid?" at your reflection in the nearest shop?

(b) Put it down to tiredness and feel glad you don't do it often?

(c) Run after the traffic warden, waving several shopping bags over your head with a criminal offence in your mind?

(d) Get in the car and cry, because this proves you can't ever be trusted on your own ever again?

This might feel entirely new. Very few of us are practised at finding out about our own inner views. What can you or I do? Quite simply – intend to be happier.

Intention is very powerful. Look behind the last thing you wanted, and got, and it's going to be sitting there. Intention.

When you decide to create a Happiness Plan, you're stating your intention to be happy, whatever life loads you with, or throws at you. The intention to be happy can fill the quiet space that exists around your life, in the reflective moments, the wondering, the internal conversations. This chapter will help you discover how to do this.

Encouragement from the person that matters most

French composer Debussy said that "music is the space between the notes". What's being played in the "space between" in your life?

When you are on a train, or in your car on the way home, what do you think about? The "space between" is the down-time between your actions, the space between your day-to-day responsibilities. For example, your background thinking, the space between the things you do on auto, the space between the conversations with your loved ones. Perhaps you don't think there is any, or much, because you are so busy, so consumed by the demands of people around you. Maybe that's worth considering in itself – who runs your life anyway?

You want to be happy? Set the intention to be happy. As strong as your intention to eat. Or sleep. Set the intention to be happy.

> **As a man thinketh, so he is.**
> Book of Proverbs

This is very precious space, this space between. But very few of us are aware of it, or influence what happens there. There's a saying that no fish is aware of the water it swims in. The space between is our equivalent. This space between can be full of goodness, in the form of encouraging thoughts. Or poisoned – by harsh self-criticism or staying trapped in past hurt. The good news is, unlike fish in water, we're able to identify what's in our space and, over time, stock it with the best content.

YOU WANT TO BE HAPPY? SET THE INTENTION TO BE HAPPY. AS STRONG AS YOUR INTENTION TO EAT. OR SLEEP. SET THE INTENTION TO BE HAPPY.

The best, best, bestest content of your space is the intention to be happy. But, like the fish and the water it swims in, it's hard to know what the "space" is. Here's something to help you find out. Imagine you are in any one of the following situations. Put yourself there, and listen to what might be playing in your space.

I'm travelling to work, stuck in traffic.
What might be playing in my space…?

My boss is describing an amazing new idea.
What might be playing in my space…?

Watching my favourite soap on the telly.
What might be playing in my space…?

The children are eating and, for once, almost quiet. I'm tidying up.
What might be playing in my space…?

My love has just gone to sleep.
What might be playing in my space…?

See what I mean? There is some space, isn't there? Now, the question is this: does your space hold negative or positive contents? Are you full of the guilt of things you need to do? Or are you playing your favourite song? Are you listening to birdsong or replaying the most hurtful dialogue from recent unresolved conflicts? What's going on?

Negative vs. positive space

You're in the car, the radio might be on. Traffic is about the same as usual. Looking out of the window, your mind starts to wander.

"Why didn't I remember to sort out his keys before I left, he'll never find them?"

"I'm looking really tired today, what was I thinking of, watching the film till 1?"

"This car – it's a nightmare."

These statements create negative space. The time with no action requiring your thought has been filled by a voice from inside your head, having a good moan, a big dig at your expense. Dr Susan Jeffers describes this voice as your inner critic in her book *Feel the Fear and Do it Anyway*. That seems a good description. The inner critic takes over your space and fills it with negative statements, which result – not surprisingly – in a less than chirpy feeling as you head down the road toward your parking space and a new working day. Allowing the negative critic access to your space in the car has not given you the best start to the day. It is allowing a backseat driver to control your life.

Or another scenario, this time you are out with your mates at an important game of rugby. You've been looking forward to this for ages, the ground is full, noisy, expectant. What's playing in your space between?

"Damn I didn't bring the camera, how stupid am I? I never remember the camera for important days – why am I turning into such a plonker?"

"Mark seems a bit off with me, did he really want me to be here?"

"I'll be in trouble at home, I always am after match day with the lads."

Or, an example of thoughts creating a positive space:

"What a fantastic atmosphere, it's great we got tickets."

"I managed to drop the kids off at swimming before we left – really good."

"How good is this, me, Steve and Mark at the final? This is the business."

Which set of thoughts is more likely to lead to enjoyment of the game?

The negative thoughts we allow in our space can have a great deal of impact on what happens in life. In one study, couples who were just about to divorce said five negative things to each other, to one positive thing. This critical communication, plus other factors such as negative body language, and harsh start ups to disagreements meant that researchers (Gottman) found they could predict divorce rates to an accuracy of 90 per cent.

This five to one ratio might be relevant in another way – do you have a five to one ratio of negative statements in your space? Would it look like this?

The Five to One Critic Ratio

1 "I'm late again, good grief. What an idiot."

2 "Why did I leave my bag at work? – I needed the memory stick."

3 "At least I did all the reading for today's meeting, and I can understand the key messages. That's good."

4 "I am always late for John's meetings – he'll not do me any favours next week when I chair the regional session."

5 "This shirt and tie look ridiculous. Why don't I ever plan my work wear?"

6 "Oh no, now I've missed the bus. Why can't I just get going in the morning?"

What is your ratio – self-criticising thoughts to self-affirming ones? OK, you can't get divorced from your self, but clearly the negative voice can still do harm if unchecked. Enough negative space creates pessimism, which in turn sets off a negative cycle which impacts attitude and behaviour. It goes something like this – take an example of a student, getting ready for an important exam.

A negative mental space

Guilty thoughts create negative space > "Why didn't I try harder?"

This leads to negative feelings > "I'm really stressed about the test"

And lowered expectations > "I'll probably just scrape through"

Which lead to less effort and will > "I'm not going to pass anyway"

Leading to poor outcomes > "I've failed the test – like I knew I would"

Which leads to guilty thoughts > "I wish I'd studied more for that test"

And the cycle goes on.

Thankfully, the opposite is also true. The positive thoughts we encourage in our space also have a great deal of impact. Enough positive thoughts create optimism, which causes good things, including better health as well as better results.

A positive mental space

Encouraging thoughts create positive space > "I think I've done my best"

This leads to positive feelings > "I'm pretty calm about the test"

And realistic expectations > "I'll probably be OK"

Which lead to a good effort and will > "I'm aiming for a good pass"

Leading to good outcomes > "I've passed the test – like I hoped"

Which leads to more encouraging thoughts > "I quite enjoyed the time studying for that test"

And the cycle goes on.

If music is the space between the notes, choosing more positive background thoughts could surround your life with a soothing melody. Or you could choose inner criticism, an endless grating like chalk down a board. The good news is, much of this is in your power to choose.

Notice what's playing in your space

If you are persuaded that positive space is a good idea, it comes down to developing a routine to get there. So what can you do? It's simple really. Figure out, in any one day, where you might have some space between. And for a while, just notice what is playing there. Take tomorrow – what's happening? When might there be a moment of downtime (see, I know what you're up against!). None at all? Don't believe you.

When you've found a few moments of downtime, just to start with, set the intention to notice what is playing. What kind of background thoughts. If you can, jot some of them down.

This is just, first of all, to identify what is happening in your space.

Exercise Spacework – identify one example of your space

Think of any journey time, maybe the time in the shower, time waiting for meetings to start, time walking the dog, time cooking dinner, waiting for Godot. Whatever.

Please think of one situation and write it down...

Your mission, should you choose to accept it, is to notice what goes through your mind, in your space, during this time. You might not notice anything at first, this exercise takes a little patience. Just be open to notice anything. Anything at all.

What did you notice playing in your space?...

Overall, was it positive or negative? Why do you say that?...

Any other examples of your space?...

What's playing there?...

Once again, is this positive or negative? …

Is there any kind of pattern emerging? …

This mental backdrop is important to your happiness. By first of all noticing what's playing in your space, you can decide whether it is positive or negative. And then, slowly, you can start to play something more enjoyable.

Make your space a happier place to be

Now you have started to notice that you do have some space, and what is currently being played there, the next exercise is to set the intention to be happy as a regular part of your space. Something that will always be there, whatever else is going on. So the normal context for your life is the intention to be happy.

So, going back to that morning story, what would the intention to be happier look like for you?

SO THE NORMAL CONTEXT FOR YOUR LIFE IS THE INTENTION TO BE HAPPY.

Intention – good breakfast, out the door with everything I need for the day.

Or

Intention – find my ruddy shoes.

Your mind will offer suggestions, give you a method based on the quality of your question. So – first one – will prompt some activity the night before, get clothes and bag ready, all good to go at 7.30am. The second one – well – under the bed mate. Thanks. Any breakfast? Nope. Where's my paperwork? No idea.

Set the intention for a happier start to the day by asking those questions. Try it.

Another source of happiness comes from the ability to be true to yourself, by having a sureness about who you are and what matters to you.

Point your life at your priorities

Getting your beliefs, your thoughts, your day-to-day life in line with who you really are – that to me is really joining the "A list". The question is how to achieve success – in relationships, your career, your choice of pastime – whatever – that also feels right. Part of your Happiness Plan is the challenge of lining up your daily actions with your innermost desires. How to find out what you really want from life, and create easy wins to test your theory out.

A couple of years ago I ran a leadership programme for some senior managers, looking at the importance of "to thine own self be true".

We asked each one of the managers three questions to help them find out more about what mattered most in terms of their values and personal priorities. See how you get on.

Question 1 – The bookstore shut-in

If you were locked inside a (safe, well stocked, facilities-rich) bookstore for an evening, and had two or three hours with no one but yourself to look after, which section, or sections of the bookshop would you love to sit down in?

Where would you go and why?

Question 2 – The prize giving

You are on stage, being awarded a great prize. Being applauded by the people you value most. Blinking out from under that spotlight – what is being awarded to you and why?

Question 3 – Your summary in Heaven

This cuts to the chase – I find it quite emotional personally.

Imagine that you have just arrived in Heaven. You are welcomed, then asked to look at your name, and the brief summary that is written next to it. The summary says the most important thing about you, in the time you were alive. What does it say?

Getting to the core of who you are can be immediate, challenging and enormously energising. I highly recommend it; because with that knowledge you are more able to create a Happiness Plan which serves your truest needs.

We're all in slightly accidental careers, feeling slightly under-qualified for the current role. That is entirely normal – for a while. Then, the question is – are you willing to take someone else's word for who you are? Achieving someone else's dream is not success. Achieving goals by sacrificing your values is not success. Feeling like a fraud, while being feted with plaudits is not success. So how can you become happier by being truer to your (say it again with me) unique, gorgeous, unprogrammable self?

Your boss says you are an excellent negotiator. Great – one part of the jigsaw.

Your children think you are their funny Daddy who makes them laugh. Another piece.

Your parents think you are their little lad who never got over his brother being a professional footballer. Another piece.

All of these add up. Most importantly perhaps, who do you say you are? What matters to you?

Please go back up to those three questions. Give them a go, then think of three adjectives to describe the true you.

Take one set of values – yours. These are the attributes you'd tell me about if I asked what is most important to you, like being honest, pioneering, saucy but honourable. Then place alongside them the day-to-day actions, the visible behaviours that people would know you for. Keith – he's a top bloke, first to the bar, last out of the cab, always looking for a way to do you a favour. Yes he's a complete online gaming timewaster, but so what? He's my best mate.

Then add to that the inner hopes and dreams that keep the cockles warm on the cold nights. That desire to someday be up on stage with Joss and Justin. To win the Nobel Prize for finding a drug that stops army boys buying unnecessary war toys and using them. The secret, delicious romance that won't let you go, buzzing your heart like espresso for beginners.

Now, how can you make sure, starting from today, that you are doing more of what matters most to you? Well, the first thing is to work it out, in a kind of logical way.

Exercise What matters most?

Question 1: What is most important to me?

■ Overall...

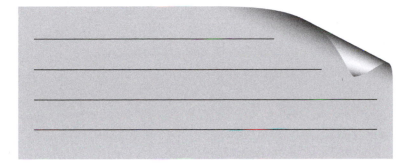

■ At work...

Question 2: What do I do all day?

■ Typical day at home – or where I spend most of my time when I'm not working. What do people see me doing?...

■ In my typical day at work – what do I do most often? What do people see me doing?...

Question 3. What ambitions or hopes do I keep secret?

■ About my whole life?...

■ About work?...

Now we've gathered that lot, how about some evaluation? For this we need a bit of perspective, so you could bravely ask someone to read this and give you honest feedback, or you could just imagine being your own best friend on this.

First of all, let's start with what you wrote about your whole life.

	My values – most important to me	The things I actually do	My dreams or hopes (secret or not)
1.			
2.			
3.			
4.			
5.			

Ten ways to get out of a bad mood

1 Eat something good for you, have some water. Bumpy moods are often because your body wants some nutrition or you are dehydrated.

2 Ask yourself "What exactly am I feeling?" Focus can reduce and soothe sometimes.

3 Close your eyes and remember the last time you felt really relaxed, happy, truly youself. Stay there for a bit. Open your eyes. Continue chairing the finance meeting.

4 Get some fresh air. In hermetically sealed buildings, go to reception and walk out the door for five minutes. Do not attempt this on remand.

5 Imagine the boss, and the boss's boss, skipping from meeting to meeting, for charity. Arrange this, see **www.magicbreakfast.com** and send the proceeds!

6 Get someone to tell you the worst joke they ever heard. Then tell it to someone who wouldn't usually hear you tell a joke, never mind a terrible one.

7 Stand up, put your arms above your head and take five deep breaths. Ask yourself "What do I need?"

8 Walk to the nearest wall, stand with your back to it and press your neck against it, so your chin touches your chest. This stretches the neck muscles and improves circulation to your brain. If your nearest wall is that of the boardroom, tell your colleagues this will improve growth in key markets.

9 Cut out the caffeine – too much caffeine stresses you out and may affect your sleep patterns too, which can make you moody. You don't have to give up tea and/or coffee entirely, buy decaffeinated varieties instead.

10 Get a magic trick from a shop. Recommended are the lit-up thumb trick or vanishing hankie. Or juggling. Practise in place of throwing heavy objects at customers. Wow children at unexpected moments.

Or just write the reason for your bad mood below.

"I'm in a really bad mood just now because..."

Or write the opposite:

"I'm in a really good mood just now because..."

All I can say about life is, oh God enjoy it!

Bob Newhart, US comedian

UNLEARN
UNHAPPINESS

04

The Happiness Plan steps

STEP 1 Decide to be happier (the ABC approach)

STEP 2 Understand happiness

STEP 3 Create a personal Happiness Plan

STEP 4 Unlearn unhappiness

STEP 5 Our plan. Make others happy

STEP 6 Some Happiness Plan examples

STEP 7 Put your plan into action

Anti-happy situations

In case you're wondering, these are the ultimate "to be avoided at all costs" obstacles to your Happiness Plan. The complete anti-thesis, ranked alongside such inverse paradigms as anti-matter, black holes and the Eurovision Song Contest. So here is my own anti-happy list (which at least gives me the outside chance of an appearance on grumpy old cheap telly) in the box opposite.

The ten greatest banes of my life

	The bane of my life	The antidote…would this make me happy?
1	Tooth problems. Root canal in particular	Happy Teeth, the follow up with penguins
2	Any kind of wilful, easily put right social injustice. Our refusal to remedy says we don't really care that much about each other (kids starting their day at school too hungry to learn, for example. (see www.magicbreakfast.com)	No hunger anywhere in the world, and they have to have a jumble sale to pay for nuclear weapons
3	Easterly winds (life-threatening to ears in all seasons)	Wear a hat
4	Good jokes told badly	Pretend to laugh
5	Once bad women turned goodly	Weep at the lost opportunity
6	Egg sandwiches containing secret onion	Dispose of using point 3
7	Misjudged financial investments (all non-food shopping, for example)	Read final section of book on controlling your finances
8	Friends you can't get in touch with (are they away, dead or just off you?)	Calling Mary Lyons
9	Hospitals in summer (no one should be anaesthetised during periods of warm sunshine)	Visit, with ice cream
10	Noticing the significant gap between what would be good to do this year, and what I will actually get around to	Don't worry, it's not over yet

Now we've got that out of the way, what about something that could seriously increase your personal capacity for happiness? Anti-happy is not the same as unhappy, it's a comfortable grumpiness. Ask your closest friends how their weekend went and I bet you find a 40–60 split between the "Really good, thanks" and "It was hellish". Try it.

Happiness is somehow suspect in our culture, so a good day out will need to be balanced with a terrible journey home; the long stretches of happy family life are bound to be punctuated with intense suffering. I am not sure why this is the case, it seems almost under the radar. Perhaps we have this "life is tough" mindset as a buffer. We have to have a low benchmark so as not to be disappointed. My advice is to set the intention for more happiness – without an equal expectation of a size nine coming down on your dreams the minute your back is turned. It could all go well – what about allowing that?

Pessimism, although comfortable, is not usually an ally in life. The more you talk the world down, the less you enjoy it. And, beyond the natural need to get a good moan off your chest, what is the point of seeing the negative all the time? I found out that optimism and pessimism can make more difference than might be thought.

CASE STUDY: OPTIMISTS VS. PESSIMISTS

A few years ago, I spent a long week facilitating a team of leaders, through the rather odd experience of making a film documentary. They all learned film basics, which was fun. They all had access to their Board level managers and colleagues for content – the idea was to make a short film about the values of the firm. And my job was to offer team insight, coaching and some leadership development along the way. Did I mention this was in a hotel inside the Arctic circle? No – someone thought that would add an element of something. Frostbite possibly.

Anyway, midst the reindeer safaris, and getting to grips with the cube in the edit suite, I noticed that the team of twenty broke down into two groups – the general optimists and the general pessimists. It didn't go along introvert/extrovert lines either – as you might think. The optimists and pessimists each had an equal level of talent, experience, management nous. But the teams were vastly different in their achievements, depending on the ratio of optimists to pessimists. Now – how do you think that might work?

In the group of pessimists – there were two different kinds of pessimism:

■ For some individuals in the group of pessimists, worrying was normal day-to-day behaviour – almost a lifestyle choice. They were often in quite a low mood, felt that the equipment was faulty, that they didn't have enough time. And very often, that the other team got support that they didn't. Their worries were not usually based on fact.

▶

- For others, pessimism was based on feelings of inadequacy, so as individuals they needed lots of support and encouragement. Those individuals were sure that they were being scrutinised by me, that I was there to report back to their superiors on their faults. Even when we were in the bar!

In the optimist team, likewise, I noticed two distinct types of optimism:

- Some of the individuals were generally in a good mood, took all problems with a shrug and were determined to enjoy the week-long programme.

- Some optimists were very keen to succeed, to win and brought their expectation of a good outcome to everything they did.

The optimists didn't always get the best outcomes. Over the course of the week, several optimists were hindered in their filmmaking by taking short cuts, by not considering all the detail that needed to happen in order to create the right conditions for the shoot, for example. So they'd lose time and do things twice. But with a good attitude – their team laughed about the disastrous attempt to interview a particularly cheerless senior manager via the internet. And they decided to keep all their out-takes – figuring their colleagues would enjoy those as much, if not more than the final film itself.

The pessimists (who made up 70 per cent of one team) were fairly cautious and did get things almost perfect, even though their film was far from ready by the allotted time. They were keen to know what would happen if they failed, if the film didn't convey the values of their firm, and if there was anything they could do ahead of time to mitigate that failure. So quite a lot of their week was spent making sure their plan noted any technical glitches, or any time their mild-mannered facilitator (that would be me) failed to give them the exact detail of their instruction. Overall, the tone was nervous, apprehensive, and as a group I'm not sure they had a lot of fun.

However, each group did make a pretty good film, and all the individuals did gain a lot of insight into how to create a more powerful team. The big difference was – you guessed it – the senior managers really enjoyed the out-takes, and judged the team containing a majority of optimists the overall event winners. Naturally the pessimists thought this was appalling. But they confessed that this was what they'd expected would happen anyway.

The ability to feel positive about the outcome of whatever task may not directly contribute to the quality of the final product – but it will significantly enhance your enjoyment of the process. You'd be right to point out that the capacity to be in a good mood, versus a worried one, is partly genetic. Some people would take a lovely two-week break if they were promised enough misery to talk about on their return. But there is a great deal you can do to steer this. Perhaps considering if you are more "pro" than "anti" might help? Being pro could mean a more positive and optimistic mindset. Being anti could mean the opposite. See how you get on with this exercise.

Quiz Do you have a generally "pro" or "anti" mindset?

1 A close member of your family rings to suggest a get-together some time next month to celebrate someone's birthday. Which would be closest to your usual reaction to such a suggestion?

(a) Don't think I can make it. Thanks anyway.

(b) Maybe, but remember how hard it was to organise the last one.

(c) Sounds great, haven't seen them in ages, let me know if you need any help.

2 As a couple, you've been together for a few years and the question of long-term commitment is starting to arise. You want to get married, but are scared to rock the boat by getting into the "Shall I ask, will they ask, don't they want to?" conversation. Valentine's Day is approaching, and she is possibly expecting a one-knee scenario. Which of the following are you most likely to be thinking?

(a) Best say I have to work late, then get home and hope she's asleep in bed.

(b) Suggest you have a chat, and say warm things about the future and hope that keeps the holding position. This isn't a good time.

(c) Time to feel the fear and buy the ring anyway.

3 You are on holiday, enjoying a day on the beach. Your partner asks if you'd like to use this week to try out a new watersport, maybe learn to water-ski or the beginners' sailing course, for example. Which would be your reaction?

(a) You're joking – do you know how expensive that would be?

(b) Maybe, but I'll want to check out all their teaching credentials and previous customer feedback. So that'll be a next holiday anyway.

(c) Why not – it'll be a laugh. I've always fancied making a fool of myself on water-skis.

4 At work, a new department is being created to look after a particular set of customers in a new, growing market. Your boss thinks you'd be good at running it and wants to know how you'd feel about taking the job as a sideways move.

(a) Why should I? The money isn't any better and who knows if it'll work?

(b) Not until I find out more. I'd like to spend a few months with the new team to find out if it would be a good fit, then I'll decide.

(c) As long as I get lots of support from the senior team, and a chance to put my stamp on it – sounds like a great opportunity.

If your response was mostly (a)s

Your natural instinct is definitely "anti". For whatever reason, you generally don't like to be pulled in new directions, offered new ideas, given a new opportunity. This could be because you don't trust people, or because the new thing is scary – which could all be quite reasonable. But you are holding yourself in a fairly negative mindset in your desire to avoid failure, being hurt or whatever else is at the core of your resistance. If you can, the next time someone suggests a new restaurant, or a new way of working they're trying out – consider saying "perhaps that could work" to move yourself gently along the spectrum. Happiness in your situation needs to be a guarded experience, which is fine; just don't rule out new sources of happiness by assuming it'll all go wrong. Trust more, worry less perhaps?

Mostly (b)s

Your natural inclination is towards being "anti" until you are sure it is the right thing to do. This is very sensible, and will minimise the amount of trouble you get into. It might be a little over-cautious though. The advice here would be to take action a little earlier, to try something out without having a 90-page web-researched report behind it. You could become gently "pro" without sacrificing everything. One way to try this would be to make a faster decision, next time you need to. On something that is reasonably low risk, say to yourself – unless I find a really good reason not to in the next 24 hours, I'll do it. That way you can be true to yourself – to have a time of cooling-off. But without the paralysis that can often happen to people who don't want to face a choice. Happiness is more likely to come from giving it a go, learning, being open to new experiences. So give yourself that chance to be happier.

Mostly (c)s

You have a very "pro" mindset, which means that you are probably really good at seeing the positive in each situation, and are willing to take risks. This positive approach to life could bring lots of new experiences and learning, and add to your sense of fulfilment and excitement. The only danger is that you jump right in, perhaps without considering all the important details before making a decision. As a way to moderate your great ebullience, perhaps contain yourself and ask "Is this really the best thing to do right now?" Action for its own sake is very addictive, so you can find yourself up a mountain on a cold weekend in January "yeah why not?" or taking care of someone else's problems just because they asked you to. Which isn't the best route to happiness either. But overall – you are probably pretty positive about life!

COULD YOU MAKE MORE ROOM FOR HAPPINESS?

Alternatively: How to be miserable

Here are the seven key strategies to sustain a lifetime of unhappiness.

Key area to work on	My current score Please rate yourself: 1 Not doing it at all. 2 Am doing it – noticeable misery increase. 3 Now second nature – state of wretched misfortune.
1 Focus exclusively on your weaknesses and the problems in your life. Make sure these problems define your public persona.	
2 In all conversations, tell as many lies as possible about who you are and what matters to you. All lies must be maintained indefinitely.	
3 Remember that life is pre-destined, therefore if you are born miserable, or poor, or with management potential, you have no choice but to accept it.	
4 Therefore, do not attempt to do anything about any bad things that happen to you or your loved ones.	

Key area to work on	My current score
	Please rate yourself: 1 Not doing it at all. 2 Am doing it – noticeable misery increase. 3 Now second nature – state of wretched misfortune.
5 Seek opportunities to hurt and humiliate the people around you. Loved ones especially. Although why you love them is a mystery. They don't love you.	
6 Ensure your mind and body are consistently unwell by, for example, avoiding sleep, decent food, fresh air and exercise. Choose vodka for re-hydration.	
7 Work excessive hours in a job that offers you no challenge, meaning or chance to save money. While in this job, work for a known bully, alongside toxic colleagues.	

Other complementary strategies to increase unhappiness

- Remind yourself that your own inadequacies are the cause of your crap life.
- Maintain total emotional denial about any serious health issues.
- Offer casual insults while making conversation.
- Maximise daily chip intake, aiming for an average two portions, hourly.

- Borrow from friends and family. Never return any loan. When asked, lie about the amounts. Spend quickly.
- Live in a damp house on a busy road.
- Wear tight, bright clothes to all formal events. Funerals especially.
- See the bad in everyone, always get your defence in first.

Follow these top tips for misery and see how bad it can get. Actually don't.

The next step is to design a happier life, starting with a better understanding of what you need, right now. Any thoughts?

Think about your needs

What if you only had to do two things in life?

1 Design a happy life, work included.
2 Make enough money to enjoy it.

And what if this came about by finding a personal definition of happiness rather than the generic "work harder, buy stuff, feel better" version. The one that encourages earning and spending and doesn't mention the other, more important bits – like making sure the ones we love are OK, happy. Like making sure our heart is OK.

I think this really *is* possible. Ambitious yes, but possible. Because in order to prioritise happiness, we have to think about ourselves in a new way – as individuals who have an expectation of happiness whatever the situation. So instead of settling in for a long dark grump when things are not going smoothly, we'd schedule in some light relief, some balm for the soul. Instead of saying "Life is tough, so I'll just have to dig in" we'd plan to balance the picture with some moments of what-ever it is that makes us happy. Going back to you, for just one more moment, what did you answer to "When and where are you happiest?" What would be the tangible difference in your life if you were able to do more of that? Not a theoretical question, I'd like you to consider it carefully.

Exercise

"If I were able to spend more time doing the things that make me happy, my life could change in the following ways…"

Thank you. It isn't beyond the realms of possibility that other people might see some improvements as well. Let's be optimistic: some bloody marvellous things could start to happen:

- We'd become reconnected with who we truly are, and what is important to us.
- We'd become kinder to ourselves, able to appreciate what we're good at, as much as the things we need to improve.
- We'd consider that we may be capable of great things, including great happiness.
- We'd stress less, worry less – with well-being as one result. There is a strong correlation between people who are physically healthy and usually happy.
- We'd look around at where we live, where our children go to school, where our food is grown. And realise that our communities need us to be concerned with each other more than guarding our individual status and our hard-earned possessions in isolation.

WE'D BECOME RECONNECTED WITH WHO WE TRULY ARE, AND WHAT IS IMPORTANT TO US.

- The richness of loving relationships would become more important.
- We'd remember that the challenge, buzz and reward of work can be great. But achieving success is often different to a sense of fulfilment.
- We'd feel that having money, or what money can buy, is essential and occasionally fabulous. But not the only answer to the question "What does it take to enjoy being alive?"

Would that make a difference in the world? What do you think?

Opening our hearts to those thoughts could lead to a potential change of personal priorities, one that would nurture our relationships, health and well-being, and, amazingly, your own needs. Your relationships and health coming first. What a thing!

When we open up our lives to the possibility of more happiness, love and fulfilment, we begin to challenge some of the assumptions that keep the world in a state. Like the need to earn so much to spend so much. The need to stay inside the sealed world of your iPod, making no eye contact, no conversation, on every journey. Or why you are not spending as much time as you'd like with your sons, or your garden, or your beloved.

You may well be thinking – good grief. Not asking much this author is she? Well this book does ask you to step outside familiar routines and consider how to upgrade the quality of your life. With some of you that should be a greater focus on happiness.

And why do I make such an outlandish claim? Simply because I've seen this happen time and time again, people becoming happier, kinder, calmer. I've seen it in organisations, in schools, to all kinds of people. I saw it as an activist, as a corporate manager, as a consultant, as a charity founder – and I've now taken to sweeping statements because it seems so important! Just deciding to live a happier life is going to start something.

What have you decided? Have you decided that you can live a happier life? Have you? Put a tick here for **yes**...

Or just chuck this book away for **no**...

Glad to see you back. Not sure if you came back via the bin or not, but anyway. Hiya.

By now you might be thinking "Fine. Marvellous. I agree to be happy. Now it's just my employer, the kids, the bank manager and the rest of the world that needs to know about it." OK. Point taken. This is not going to be without some need for stakeholder management! The Happiness Plan you'll design for yourself is definitely a win–win with the ones you love/tolerate/pay huge amounts to every month.

So that's my little theory. Designing a happy life is the next step for those of us able to make space for it. Living a happy life on purpose, not hoping that we get the odd fleeting moment of bliss when your team avoids relegation, the train actually reaches the station, when your time at the office feels like something you actually look forward to.

Ten things to start if you want to be happier

1 Smile more – no really. It somehow perks your brain up. And (mostly) looks nicer.

2 Feel that you are the one responsible for today being a good or bad one (not the boss, the cat or the weatherman).

3 Trust more – expect people to want to help you.

4 Be kind to yourself, say encouraging things rather than having a go all the time.

5 Look around at what you've already got, rather than what you need.

6 Ask people "Can I help you?" Obviously with some context. Not randomly.

7 Take care of basics (go to bed earlier, eat better, get some air and exercise).

8 Look at how far you've come at something you are proud of doing.

9 Ask your best friend what she/he would like to do for a treat.

10 Work out one thing you enjoy about your job, and think about how it would make your customers/colleagues happier if you did more of it.

Cut to the chase. *"Can I be happier?"*

Yes.

Just checking.

Your newest habit: happiness.

Happiness is a bit like good health. Both get created, quietly, while you're busy doing other things. Take good health. If you choose some simple steps on a regular basis, then – unforeseen bad things aside – you could expect a reasonable standard of wellness. You become a creature of good habits. Habits to improve your health might be:

■ Understanding what triggers your headaches and take action (NB – for migraine, common triggers are red wine, chocolate, cheese. So avoid these. For headaches caused by head injury drink more water, increase sleep, reduce computer screen time. Get your eyes checked.)

■ Doing a reasonable amount of exercise.

■ Choosing exercise that won't kill you (don't try to go up the mountain at +20 stone for example).

■ Getting enough sleep.

■ Eating and drinking in moderation, apart from the odd essential large one.

So good health could be about an easy routine where exercise, sleep and good food are just normal and everyday. Could the same thinking apply to happiness? Is it possible to create a routine that gently made sure you could be as happy as possible? Or is that trying to plan the unpredictable?

A PLAN FOR PERSONAL HEALTH

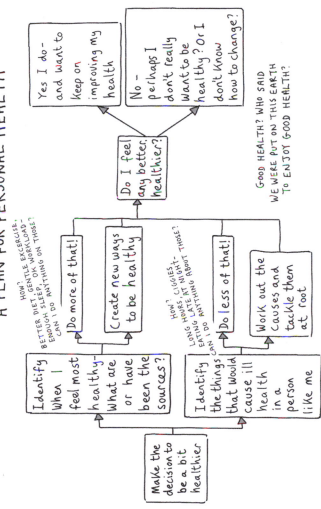

A plan for personal health

A PLAN FOR PERSONAL HAPPINESS

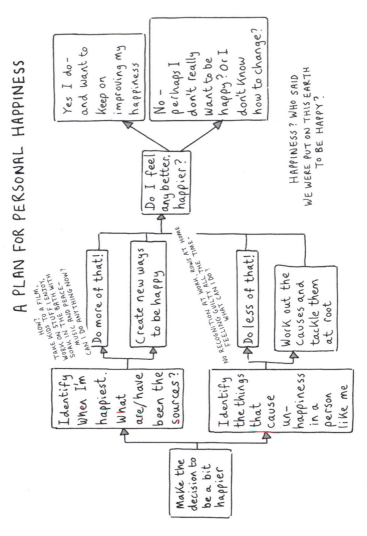

A plan for personal happiness

Habits can either support your Happiness Plan or undermine it. Supportive habits I'll come to in a moment, but what about the saboteurs? Habits like a belief in stress, or procrastination. Perhaps victimhood is another kind of habit – something goes wrong because "they" did it. In some ways, increasing happiness is about identifying the most successful of your internal saboteurs, those that have established themselves as normal, routine, and then gently learning to do something different.

How can you get out of a bad habit? Ask the Mother Superior for a new one? Er, no. You get rid of a bad habit by understanding why it's there. For example, with procrastination it's normally based on fear of getting it wrong. The steps are to ask yourself why you procrastinate. Why do you leave everything to the last minute, look at urgent emails and close them without taking action, fail to follow up after important meetings?

The fear angle says that it is better to ignore the harder things than get them wrong. Your Happiness Plan is to ask why that kind of sabotage is even getting the microphone. And then ABC it. The happiness here would be to get things done, over, as soon as they possibly can be.

YOU GET RID OF A BAD HABIT BY UNDERSTANDING WHY IT'S THERE.

What's Your Happiness Plan?

Give up procrastinating, probably not yet though!

Seriously, I'd be a lot happier if I got things done as soon as I could. Stop carting work to and from home and feeling guilty. Happiness is a finished paper.
Marian, medical researcher

There are two ways to view this. One is that you procrastinate because you always have. It is now what you do, and you are known for it. So, hey – there we are. Second way is to use the ABC of happiness technique to change it. This is the one you will want to choose, but not today because you're a bit busy. Remember the technique?

What's Your Happiness Plan?

My sense of happiness is vicarious. I make myself happier if I can make the other people in my life happier: according to a hierarchy of family, friends, working up to total strangers. It's an impossible aim as they're likely to be as conflicted as me, also as immune to being happy, but it's always good to try. I'm not religious but note this philosophy is key to Christianity, Buddhism and Islam so it's not unique.
James, freelance web designer

Step A: Allow more room for happiness

Can you imagine what life would be like if, instead of procrastinating, you got things done and out of the way by taking action as soon as you can, by offloading impossible work or getting help? Can you figure out why you're not able to do more at the time? It could be because you are simply overloaded.

Step B: Begin – start the change

For example, tackle incoming mail as soon as it arrives. Just one item first – then notice how it makes you feel. Pretty good? Now, get to the scariest part. Have you turned any procrastinated-over tasks into monsters yet? Left them for so long that they're now so urgent, they are now untouchable. Get help, sit down with a colleague and work out if they still have to be done, and how. It is likely that a simple update call is all that's needed – in the real world that is. In your mind you're already going to prison.

That's the power of procrastinations – it keeps you permanently held down by guilt. The book *Taming Your Gremlin*[10] is a good resource if you want to delve further into the reasons.

Step C: Continue – until happier

Keep going. Create a goal of no more monster tasks and no inbox with 2000 unread messages. Congratulate yourself on every bit of progress. You have now decided not to co-operate with the part of your self that wants to feel in trouble, guilty and secretive.

[10] Rick Carson, *Taming Your Gremlin: a Surprisingly Simple Method for Getting Your Own Way* (Quill, 2003).

NATIVE WISDOM

There is an old Cherokee story about a tribal elder who is teaching his grandson about life. "A fight is going on inside me," he said to the boy. "It is a terrible fight and it is between two wolves.

"One is evil – he is anger, envy, sorrow, regret, greed, arrogance, self-pity, guilt, resentment, inferiority, lies, false pride, superiority and ego.

"The other is good – he is joy, peace, love, hope, serenity, humility, kindness, benevolence, empathy, generosity, truth, compassion and faith.

"The same fight is going on inside you – and inside every other person too."

The grandson thought about it for a minute and then asked his grandfather, "Which wolf will win?"

The old Cherokee simply replied "The one you feed."

Source: Michael Neill, *Feel Happy Now* (Hay, 2007)

It seems to me that there are seven areas where a happiness-forming habit could make a big difference to life quality. I'm basing these on the existing research and my experience working on personal change with groups and with individuals over fifteen (long) years. I could go as far as to say that both happiness and misery are habit related.

The seven habits of highly happy people

(OK, OK)

1 **Encourage yourself.** Specifically, re-stock your mental space with encouragement. Earlier in the book we considered the "inner critic" – the voice inside your head which can encourage or demoralise you. Every time you hear the critic swing into action, interrupt with a word of encouragement. Yes – this could take time! For example, respond kindly to mistakes or imperfections (yours as much as those of others). So what if she screwed up, forgot, spilled it? It needn't open the floodgates.

2 **Seize the Carp. Em.** Stay in the here and now. Happiness is a feeling – more powerfully enjoyed while you are in the present moment. Do you spend your time replaying the events of last weekend, or wondering about what to do next week? Today is where the fun is more likely to be. The carp is here, now, today. You know what I mean.

3 **Do something you are good at, and enjoy, every day.** A few chords on your guitar, the ferocious interrogation of financial data, the quiet word of encouragement for your daughter. Play to your strengths and do something that makes you feel wonderful – or nearly – every day. Remind youself of your strengths.

4 **Notice the small good things, fully.** Even on a rubbish day, something good will happen. Many of us push our way through the hours with nary a glance at the flowers in full

bloom – and yet it is the small, seemingly insignificant moments that make the big picture work. It might be as small as a good cup of tea, but noticing and appreciating it will make a difference.

5 **Let your family and friends know you love them.** This needn't be a big deal, just something to remind your loved ones that they matter to you. One phone call? The quality of your close relationships is a big indicator of your overall happiness. Find a way to make others happy.

6 **Release it. Not the budgie or the boss, no.** In every life there is a build-up of pressure, or longing, or the urge to express. Release should ideally be proportional to pressure. So, five tough report updates this week equals five shockingly wonderful massages, or five great bike rides through the woods, or five ice creams. Unthinkable, right? Release is a happiness habit designed to stretch your comfort zone. Marvellous.

7 **Enjoy yourself.** The physical needs have really got to be met. No not just those, thank you. The tangible thrill of being alive in nature, enjoying the elements, enjoying a thrilling kiss from your beloved, signing up for all sorts of fun. If you don't rinse your soul in a deep green place regularly, what's the point? Consider this. All the great faiths pay their god of choice homage for giving us humans the ability to feel pleasure, to exult in our physical bodies. Whether you see your body as the housing for a divine spirit, or as the best little dancer in Leicester. Enjoy your physical self. We're built for pleasure.

Did I repeat the message to enjoy yourself? Good.

Setting up a habit isn't easy. If you drive, you'll sometimes get home without really remembering which decisions you took, or the tangible sensations of changing gear, looking in the mirror. Why? Because you have learned to drive, and had enough practice for the basics to become habit. You get home on a kind of auto-pilot. I mean auto-pilot as a state of awareness which includes high focus on the traffic – but not on each individual action to control the car. If this was a book by a biologist, this is where you'd get a brain diagram. Instead...

Habits. A very good way to gradually grow a positive, enjoyable way of thinking. Which, over time, could become as instinctive as driving up the road. A habit grows from repeated action, creating neural networks in our brain that can direct our actions as well as do other things without conscious thought.

Repeated action will inevitably result from a belief. The belief that it is possible to drive (apart from the lack of regular buses where you live, perhaps) can propel you to learn to drive, to keep learning, to pass the test and then drive to work. This is an important point, because many of us lead lives with some element of routine, and our habits are likely to shape and quantify the amount of happiness – or quiet desperation or outright misery – that we enjoy/endure. In that way, our thoughts also determine how we feel.

HABITS. A VERY GOOD WAY TO GRADUALLY GROW A POSITIVE, ENJOYABLE WAY OF THINKING.

Here I should point out that we learn and internalise bad habits with just as much skill as good habits. A habit of saying "oh don't worry, I'll do that" when the boss needs photocopies at 6pm. That's the "others matter more than me" way of thinking that leads to all sorts of bother. Irish/Jewish mothers are experts at this. How many Irish mothers does it take to change a light bulb? "Don't worry about me, I'm fine here in the dark"… If your belief – perhaps from your early family life – has been that you are good at looking after people, the thought pattern or belief could lead to the following kinds of actions:

- Listening, offering advice without ever asking for any support when *you* need it.
- Giving up your only time off to see family – because you should.
- Putting work deadlines ahead of some restful time off – because they need you to work on something.

Over time, the pattern of looking after everyone else and not looking after yourself erodes self-esteem and self-confidence, which can then lead to all sorts of emotional withdrawal.

But is it possible to identify misery-making habits, or replace them with something healthier? Well, if belief forms the basis

How beliefs create action, then habits

Important area of my life	What is the desired outcome to improve happiness?	What habit could support that outcome?	What action could be taken regularly to form a habit?	A happier belief that could prompt an action
Health	To have more energy, through a healthier diet	I now have a good lunch at work, so I am not really hungry and eating junk food on the way home	I've looked into good local places for lunch, near where I work	I seem to feel better in myself when I eat at the right times in the day
Close relationship	That we go on a "hot date" once a month – we both know it's important	I book a babysitter and arrange the evening	We had a chat and realised we just don't have romantic time together any more	I love my partner, our love affair is so important to look after
Work	It feels great to be recognised for my hard work sometimes	When I get something done that makes a big impact with customers, I let my colleagues know – gently	I make sure my reports are based on what our customers say they want – not what we want to sell them	I really get a buzz from profitable, open and honest customer relationships

of action, which if repeated enough times becomes habits, it might be possible to reverse-engineer from happier habits backwards, to understand the actions you could choose everyday, to give yourself the chance of more happiness-creating thoughts. Worth a try?

The negative habit of pressure

One route to a happier life is to identify the biggest sources of pressure – both internal and external. External pressure could be a work deadline, a home improvement project that suddenly becomes a builder-free zone, or an important exam. An internal source of pressure could be critical thoughts, fear or raised expectations.

For example, the school reunion. Maybe just a chance to see old friends, laugh about the old days and be amazed at how small your ex-teachers are. Or else a chance to wreak havoc on your self-esteem by imagining each ex-classmate to be super successful at work, and the architect of a perfect family at home. Despite your own considerable achievements, the internal pressure caused by comparing and competing thoughts could become unbearable – everyone else has done so well and just look at *your* life, etc. Internal pressure from this kind of thinking can cause a whole range of distress, and can become a real barrier to happiness.

So what can be done? The next part of the Happiness Plan will focus on a way to reduce those internal sources of pressure by changing some of the most intensely self-pressuring thoughts into something more gentle, more encouraging. Like you, only a happier version!

This is a three-step process, creating happiness from the inside out. If you like.

1 You learn how to think fewer self-critical, comparing, competing thoughts. Which creates …

2 A less pressured, more self-encouraging way of thinking. Which leads to …

3 A more tolerant, emotionally stable reaction to life's events.

Now, being unique and gorgeous humans, we each have our own setting for internal pressure – we are all on a spectrum. One of my ex-work colleagues is amazingly good at self-encouragement (I sometimes wonder if there is a gender angle on this – what do you think?). So, when faced, as we once were, by technical melt-down on the morning of a big client presentation, his first thoughts were – hey, even if none of the slides are available, we'll still blow them away with what we've got to say. The rest of the team, me included, were convinced that our USP lay hidden somewhere between slides 9 and 20, and only the miracle that is PowerPoint could save the day. Oh, and we all self-berated for England on how we could have saved a copy late last night, brought another laptop, etc.

That example shows opposite ends of the self-pressuring thoughts spectrum – my male colleague feeling no internal pressure, the rest of us reeling from it! So, is there a spectrum of internal pressure, a way to identify where you and I might live, most of the time, in terms of our habitual reaction to life's events?

In order to find out, maybe scoring levels of self-criticism vs. self-encouragement on this spectrum might be useful, if not scientific. Imagine that a factual, dispassionate way to analyse any problem, or any event scored zero – neither positive nor negative.

Then imagine that each level of self-criticism scored from minus 1 (mildly self-critical) to minus 5 (wildly self-critical). And that each level of self-encouragement scored from plus 1 (mildly self-encouraging) to plus 5 (wildly self-encouraging). As shown on the diagram below.

Clearly life at minus or plus five is not going to be a good place; minus five is fraught with self-criticism, while plus five is close to selfish narcissism. The goal, I suppose, is to live either side of zero, preferably on the plus side. What do you think? Would it be good to have a plan to get you on your own plus side?

The skill, in terms of your Happiness Plan, would be to see where you are, and what can be done to be in the best possible place.

MINUS 5 = WILDLY
SELF-CRITICAL

"I nearly always judge myself harshly when things go wrong, I'm good at blaming myself"

PLUS 5 = WILDLY
SELF-ENCOURAGING

"I never blame myself when things go wrong, I usually blame circumstances or others"

$$-5 \quad -4 \quad -3 \quad -2 \quad -1 \quad 0 \quad +1 \quad +2 \quad +3 \quad +4 \quad +5$$

ZERO = PERSONAL EQUILIBRIUM

"When things go wrong I don't judge myself over harshly, nor do I let myself off the hook. I try to consider the facts and take a decision"

Are you self-critical or self-encouraging?

Where do you think you are on that scale?

Is that where you'd like to be? If not, where would you prefer to be?

The positive habit: living in the present

A work colleague recently said to me – I know why my wife is never particularly happy. She is always either living in the past, revisiting old battles, or off in the future, worrying about what might happen.

This struck me as being quite powerful – the idea that happiness really can only be felt, not thought. And that only exists in the here and now.

Trouble is, we all get into the habit of bouncing over life's events, moving on, not particularly engaging with what is before us. Either because of the lure of the past or the future, or because we're afraid of what is going on here and now. The habit of living here and now is a good idea – but perhaps it might be easier to understand by looking at the opposite. Skimming over life. This is a concept I first introduced in an earlier book (*Soultrader*, Momentum 2002) and seems useful to revisit here.

It is hard to feel happiness if you don't regularly practise being in the present, being emotionally alert to this moment, right now. The opposite of being emotionally present in the here and now is skimming. Skimming means staying on the top of each situation, never really immersing yourself emotionally, intellectually. Skimming through each big life event, ever so slightly wanting it to be over. What's next? Skimming is not daring to do it properly now in case you get it wrong. Buying skimmed milk because you ought to and hating every drop. Putting the thing you most want to do at number 11 on a list of 10. Deferring gratification until long after the moment has gone. You could be here, in this kiss, in this moment of congratulation, in this warm sea on a warm day. Or you could keep yourself emotionally suspended, somewhere else, somewhere in your head, not your heart. This habit can really thwart your happiness – without you even knowing it.

Skimmers wait until they feel better placed to enjoy all the soft fruit of a happy life. It isn't going to happen. Believe me. Skimmers will stand on stage, with an adoring crowd, but vaguely worrying how they'll get home afterwards. Skimming through life's events versus being in the here and now. Which do you think more likely to make you happy?

Soulskimmers live on the surface of life's rich experience, just waiting to be happy, but not right now. Might you be having a quiet skim right here and now?

Quiz Do you engage with life or skim over it?

Answer a, b or c to the following:

1 You work hard for days to get a report done. The boss comes over and starts to say, "Marion, this is great". Ignoring the fact that your name is Wendy, which answer is your most normal reaction?

   (a) Start humming a little tune in your head and look down until he goes away?

(b) Look him in the eyes and smile warmly to let him know you are glad to be recognised for the hard work?

(c) Stand up, spill coffee on desk contents and mutter "it was nothing" while mopping frantically?

2 Your team get the chance to present at the annual leadership event, do you:

(a) Have flu that week?

(b) Get the team together to work on the piece, ahead of time?

(c) Ignore it until one week before, then panic and put together something painfully stressful for the day?

3 At your best friend's housewarming party, do you:

(a) Create a private space behind bunting and read his old *GQ* magazines?

(b) Get to know what is happening in the lives of your old friends?

(c) Get drunk, fall into the faux fireplace and cause the planned DIY/repair weekend to happen a month early?

4 When reading an article about your specialist field of work, do you:

(a) Think, blimey I could have written something on that, then forget it immediately?

(b) Note the email and send the author a note to arrange lunch to compare approaches?

(c) Doodle a handlebar 'tache and pointy ears on her photo?

If you answered mostly (a)s

You are probably an introvert skimmer, creating as little fuss as possible, yet probably wanting to achieve huge amounts. Your need to stay in your comfort zone is growing by the day. The Happiness Plan response is to perhaps think that all you fear doesn't actually exist in the world outside your head. The question is, when do you plan to take the brakes off your journey to success by first of realising you do a great job, and that your friends love you? It's true.

Mostly (b)s

You come across as someone who wants to live in the moment and enjoy it. This is great – and you don't need anyone to tell you. Make sure you also help those who are not as clued in as you. The sin of smug is the worst one.

Mostly (c)s

Apart from being an extrovert skimmer, you are potentially on a collision course for the rest of your life. The goal would be to have a day or two with the phrase "I like who I am" in the back of your mind. Alternatively, staying home?

How to live in this moment – Reduce your skim rate

So how can we be more emotionally alert in this present moment?

A potential future skim event	What you could do
Your appraisal	You remember when. You prepare. You make sure the boss knows what you have done. You say what you want to do next.
Your next job	You hear about it. You phone straight away. You find out what they want and you send a letter today, saying how you could help. You expect to get it. You research. You tell them why you can help in the interview. You get the job.
Chance to tell the boss's boss your ideas. Can you be bothered?	Your boss's boss is always looking for good ideas, and you've got one. He was once where you are. You tell him.
Your redundancy	They are going to downsize your department. You phone HR and arrange an early chat. And do your home finances – how much you need each month and your marketable skills. You figure a time to go, with 3 months' jobsearch. You see HR, suggest a leaving date, negotiate some retraining. They agree, seem helpful. No one else has talked to them. It's hard, but you're calling the shots.
Do nothing days, followed by major guilt, whizzing through without as much care as should be there	You have worked out what you want to make happen. And day-to-day priorities feel reasonably clear. So though you can't always get them all done, you are mostly pleased with progress.

A potential future skim event	What you could do
You can't remember what happens next, career wise	You keep talking to people and testing ideas about what might open up next. You keep an open mind on being successful at this, or something else that feels right.
Your life	You are emotionally and mentally as well as physically present while it happens.

Skimmers have a habit of skimming. It becomes normal, easy. This is who I am. I skim. That's it.

Might it help to forward-plan your next month to kick the skim habit? OK. What we need to do is find out the next significant event (e.g. a presentation, appraisal, interview, client meeting whatever it is that you are dreading and happy about in the diary – you know what it is). Get out your diary (your fancy phone or your bit of paper, whatever) and write the following. Yes it can also apply to the big date/family event/parent evening!

On each one of these, there is a skim option. Which is as follows:

■ Forget all about it
■ Have a major last-minute panic
■ Try bluffing on the day
■ Suffer post-event regret, low self-esteem and punishing of anything in range, e.g. dogs or small children
■ Of course causing the brain to try to forget the next time (and ladies and gentlemen, a pattern is born!).

Today's date...

Significant events coming up this week:

1 ....

2 ....

Next week:

1 ....

2 ....

Next month:

1 ....

2 ....

Does that sound familiar? Take a look at this week. Are you planning to give that number 1 event a good big skim? OK – fine we all do it. And while these patterns don't change overnight, your desire to improve things for yourself is something you can do in an instant. A millisecond now could put something quite amazing in motion. Really.

You have choice, you can choose the option most likely to lead to happiness, success and fulfilment – the opposite of the skim option. Right now. All you have to do is look at the significant events in your diary. You have the choice to look in your diary now or just say, forget it, can't be bothered ... fine here. Against each one, you

- Check it out in advance
- Figure out the desired outcome
- Be awake and alert during the event
- Record some of the things you get from it
- Follow through.

What language do you naturally think in – engaging with or skimming past? Take one event, in one week, and find out what a big difference this choice will make. Your Happiness Plan might work better with you around!

The habit. "A kinder impulse to deal with mistakes or signs of human imperfection..."

What a wonderful aspiration. Can you imagine the pay-off if you could learn to tolerate the mistakes and imperfections of others to a higher degree than you do now? It doesn't mean downtrodden, or immune to anger – it might mean a more measured response to life's day-to-day challenges.

What regular action could cause that to become one of your personal happiness habits? One example. Could you imagine a new version of a regular front-room incident? Next time little Sam spills a sugary drink on the carpet, your first reaction is "It's OK love, it's only an accident". Mop drink, cuddle child, blood pressure stable. Slightly different from the normal yells, tears and Stain Devil/blood pressure emergency, perhaps?

Or could you manage "Don't worry, these things happen" next time your beloved locks the car keys inside the car? OK, your bag and phone are in there and this is the second time this year. What would that "don't worry" reaction be like? Impossible? Possible but only with deep breathing/sedation? Certainly the gentler reaction is more conducive to a call to the garage and quick sort out than World War IV in the car park. Or you could choose twenty minutes of "How could you be so stupid?" ending with the less than ideal engagement-cancelling situation and belated apology. Sorry, I do love you really.

So these gentle responses – the ability to state something to diffuse the difficult situation, rather than inflame it – are based on what? On a belief that we are all doing our best. Sometimes we screw up, but it's no big deal. It's only a big deal if you get really upset about it. Can you consider that as something you really believe? "We all screw up, it's part of being human. It's just an accident."

SOMETIMES WE SCREW UP, BUT IT'S NO BIG DEAL. IT'S ONLY A BIG DEAL IF YOU GET REALLY UPSET ABOUT IT.

Obstacles to happiness. Have you chosen a stress-based approach to life?

Have you set up a stress-based approach to life? Well, have you? I haven't got all day you know. Come on, come on. Oh, sorry, I got a bit stressed there.

Students in most countries get a range of exam grades, from A to F. In most cultures, the A grades get but a passing mention compared to the F grades – they are after all the ones that need improvement. But it does mean that the education process focuses almost all attention on the weaknesses, rather than the strengths, of the individual. The student rarely feels praised, just told to improve. This carries on through employment; many employees feel they get little recognition, never mind praise in the workplace.

Given this early training we receive in focusing on our weaknesses rather than strengths, is it any wonder we develop self-critical thinking as the norm? Or that we see life as a series of stressful events to somehow be got through?

Is it possible that you could be looking at your life through the prism of stress or self-criticism? For example, if you are planning to talk to someone about your finances (a bank manager say), you might go in for the conversation with any of the following mindsets:

"I am so crap with money, I'll have to hope the bank manager takes pity on me." (a self-critical approach)

Or

"If I don't get this loan, this means the end of my flat and my whole life is going to fall apart." (the stress approach)

Now, given that the banks are very very keen to sell us money at a high rate of interest, this might not be the hardest example, but I hope you see what I mean. There are other ways to consider the trip to the bank.

A self-encouraging mindset might be:

"I'm hopeful that the bank manager will approve this loan – I've given him all the supporting documents and we've had a good talk on the phone."

A lower-stress approach might be:

"If I get this loan, it'll be great but if I don't, I've got room to reduce some outgoings – it won't be the end of the world."

In terms of the bank manager experience, which would you prefer? And which would produce the more desirable outcome?

Self encouragement, rather than self-criticism is the core of your Happiness Plan.

Make other people happy

The other day I was speaking at an event, telling people about the BoB strategy. First of all I asked, "What do you think a BoB strategy is going to be about?" Someone stuck their hand up and said "Can we fix it? Yes we can". I liked that, so that's my new BoB strategy. But let me tell you a bit about the original one.

The BoB strategy is a way to get the Best of Both (aha) in any situation. It seems to me that problems arise when people are polarised into different camps. You are this or that – stark, polarised, non-negotiable. Take the private and public sector for example. You are either a private sector or a public sector type of person, I've been told. Either a profit-seeking shark or a slow-mo tree hugger. That doesn't seem quite right does it? Many private sector firms are trying to do their profit-making thing in a way that builds more stakeholder trust. Trying hard to get competitive advantage by being seen to have values and do the right thing by the community/environment/employees. And most public sector firms are seeking ways to trade, create revenue, reduce the bureaucracy in favour of action. So the organisation that decides to put BoB at the heart of their growth strategy gets to put speed to market alongside trust. Social enterprise is a great example of this – creating social improvements using a business practice approach.

The stark divide of left/right, private/public, student/employee – whatever – seems to cause more problems than it solves. Being a human is a natural coalition, lots of messy diverse forces acting in union to cause you to make your choices. And so much unhappiness seems to come from the need to cling to an identity that stays stuck on, whatever. We all evolve, change, develop – our human lives are simply the transition from here and now to a future where we hope to be happier – with whatever views. Are you wearing your rigid identity today?

Our sexuality is another contender for "stick a label on, doesn't matter if it makes them miserable". Gay/straight. Mostly clear, not always. People fall in love without a guide-book to romance and, in a society with less prejudice, feel able to fall in love with a person, not a gender. It just seems more important to glory in uniqueness and take the Best of Both options on offer. Less off-the-shelf and structured perhaps – so sorry if this recommendation is out of your comfort zone. My firm advice is that you check BoB out, and order double happy portions, twice, on the way.

... for more happiness at work

For example, at work. What makes you happy there? Never thought about it? Why don't you think about it? We spend way too many hours, on average, doing the best we can for the best we can earn, and happiness is an afterthought?

I know we had a brief look at this earlier, but with the Best of Both in mind, is it possible that you are, once again, encamped? I hear universities would be great places if it wasn't for the students. Libraries if it wasn't for the readers. Your place of work – any them and us there? Are you restricting your workplace happiness to membership of the senior team? Or "anything as long as I'm not called admin"?

For now, please just think about the top five things – you go home from work in a great mood when these things have happened. These are things you really enjoy.

The things I enjoy most in my work

1 ....

2 ....

3 ....

4 ....

5 ....

Now, if you've written 5.30 Friday next to number 1 and cut and pasted through to number 5, I've got to tell you something. Leave.

When you consider those things at work – great. Are any of those good for your customers or clients? Which ones are most useful? Can you make sure you major on those – design a job where you make the customers cock-a-hoop doing things that make you happy? I said cock-a-hoop.

Picture the scene. Your hard pressed, decent sort of boss gets an email (not the usual e-maul) from you with the following suggestion:

Jo,

Now we've finished the **Big Inc** project, I've been looking over the client file and thinking more about what makes these clients happy. Looking at their satisfaction surveys, plus my experience with them over the past two years, it seems they really appreciate it when we give them feedback on their strategy rather than just turn it into a nice presentation for the investors. This has to be done with care, obviously, but I'd like to look at how we can offer them more value add in this area. As you know, I've been keen to develop my strategy skills so this might be a nice win/win. What are your thoughts?

Steve.

Steve,

Thanks. Go for it.

Don't forget my finance report due 2.00.

Jo

Steve designs a piece of work that makes him happy and potentially makes the clients even happier. No boss in my world would have turned that down. If yours would, hold a peaceful coup and suggest he/she spend more time with the fax machine. You don't have a fax machine anymore? Exactly!

Obviously we'll need to add a layer of management language, targets and stuff to keep the unsuitablesuitabove happyish. But still, perhaps mapping the happy would work for you. Using the idea of finding the Best of Both.

"Out of my top five. The ones that make our clients/customers happiest are..."

1 ....

2 ....

3 ....

4 ....

5 ....

So this is how that might look, as a picture.

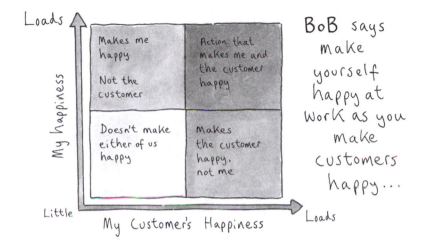

Loads

Makes me happy

Not the customer

Action that makes me and the customer happy

My Happiness

Doesn't make either of us happy

Makes the customer happy. not me

Little

My Customer's Happiness

Loads

BoB says make yourself happy at work as you make customers happy...

The purpose of our existence is to seek happiness.

His Holiness The Dalai Lama

OUR PLAN: MAKE OTHERS HAPPY

05

The Happiness Plan steps

STEP 1 — Decide to be happier (the ABC approach)

STEP 2 — Understand happiness

STEP 3 — Create a personal Happiness Plan

STEP 4 — Unlearn unhappiness

STEP 5 — **Our plan. Make others happy**

STEP 6 — Some Happiness Plan examples

STEP 7 — Put your plan into action

A win–win solution

Lasting happiness comes from finding the win–win with others. This means understanding your sources of happiness, and theirs; then making a home in the overlap. OK, you could say that happiness doesn't involve others. Fine – happiness is getting away from the madding crowd. Or reading, with no company and a very cosy fire, thank you very much. Of course there are areas of private and personal pleasure – thank goodness. But when it comes to setting up big, healthy chunks of happiness in your life, my advice is to consider this: **How can I be happy, in a way that also makes them happy?**

Them being – colleagues at work, key domestic stakeholders (I jest... let's call them children) and anyone else in your life. You become happier when they become happier. Does that sound saintly? Not humanly possible?

In my view we've grown an imbalance – we strive towards individual achievement sometimes neglecting our human desire to share and belong. While our workplace leaders convince themselves we're there for the cash and status, survey after survey shows we prize the social elements of our work. So, if work becomes a win–win, perhaps it allows you to enjoy that sense of connection, to deepen relationships – as the psychologists keep telling us, the key to happiness!

How to be happier at work

Whatever your outlook, the first step to increase your happiness at work is to ABC it. To first of all allow that there could be more happiness on offer. Could you allow the fact that your job could make you happy?

For example, could you work out what you enjoy most in any one day? Then work out why that also helps someone else achieve their goals? You could then make the case for doing more of what you enjoy – which might be a good starting place for more happiness.

Going back to the ABC model, perhaps you could allow some room for happiness at work, then begin to do more of the work you enjoy – and continue with the nice external win–win to keep the boss happy!

A Could you **A**llow more room for happiness at work?

B What would you start with – then **B**egin

C And **C**ontinue. It may well make you happier…

Ways of thinking about work

- Work is never fun.
- Work requires a boss.
- Work is something to be endured for forty years.

Or

- Work is doing what you love and being paid for it.
- Your desk is a springboard for future success.
- Work can be negotiated to fit family needs.

Which one is more you?

You're meant to be happy at work. True or false? If your answer is "false" that's understandable. Many of us grew up with the idea that work is to be endured, rather than enjoyed. Or maybe you can honestly answer – true. In which case you're about to agree with a few paragraphs.

YOU'RE MEANT TO BE HAPPY AT WORK. TRUE OR FALSE?

We'll leave aside all the glorious marketing about work being the most important thing in life, the way to a glorious, financially smug future and lots of cars. Work is important, but as the area of our lives where we perhaps have less control, increasing the levels of happiness is going to be a bit of a challenge. Many of us give up on it. Work to live or live to work, they say? And I put my glass down and head back to do emails.

Workplace happiness can come from any or all of the following sources:

- The work itself – the intrinsic motivation
- The social aspects – colleagues and friends with common purpose
- The rewards – travel, a car, prestige, increased aspiration – extrinsic motivators
- The sense of purpose and meaning – particularly in vocational jobs
- The learning – developing new skills and being able to grow confidence in applying them.

It might be useful to just check back on your reasons for wanting to do your current job. What did you expect to gain – and is your motivation still the same? Does your job now feel more routine, something you do purely for the security and perhaps limited financial reward?

Source: City & Guilds Happiness Index 2007, www.cityandguilds.com

CITY & GUILDS REVEALS UK'S HAPPIEST WORKERS

City & Guilds, the UK's leading authority on work-related education and training issues, compiles the Happiness Index every year, tracking the satisfaction and fulfilment of the country's workforce.

The 2007 Happiness Index surveyed 1,000 UK employees, revealing that nearly a third of people (32 per cent) said they were not particularly happy at work – giving a satisfaction rating of less than 7 out of 10. At the bottom of the pile are HR managers (2 per cent), lawyers (4 per cent) and secretaries (4 per cent).

However, it's not all bad news, as the Happiness Index also reveals a more contented side to our British workforce with the dawn of a new workday bringing joy to hairdressers. A cheerful 57 per cent admitted they look forward to returning to work after a day off.

The nation's happy coiffeurs are closely followed by beauty therapists, early years and childcare workers and plumbers.

Top ten list on how to be happy at work (whistling is optional)

1 Work! Do the job. Do it with all you've got and if you can't, consider why. If you are a square peg in a round hole, ask for help. If you've taken to hiding in the loo after lunch, this is a clue.

2 Imagine you couldn't do it any more. If someone told you the firm was packing up and moving to Bangkok, without you, what would you miss? This odd perspective might identify things you actually enjoy (if nothing springs to mind, this could be the little push you need to consider moving on ... though not to Bangkok, obviously).

3 Can you be true to yourself at work? Or do you have to put on an act? If you have to smile on demand, or pretend to be happy, something inside you is dying. Find out how to be yourself and if that isn't possible, consider moving on. (Does anyone stay in the same job at the end of this top ten?)

4 See the big picture – what is the purpose of where you work? Understanding the big picture will help you decode the boss's rather strange requests.

5 How does your job fit into that big purpose? Do you know the link between your desk and happy customers/users?

6 If you have no idea, you need to find out. What is your unique contribution to the organisation? Why is that valuable?

7 How much choice do you have in your job? For example, can you choose how much development you receive? Or when to present your ideas to the boss? The level of control you have over the direction of your role is closely linked to the level of choice you believe you have.

8 Give something away everyday; not the Tippex, no. Your fulfilment at work is directly linked to how much you contribute. Funny that. So – does anyone need your help? How does "Can I help you" sound?

9 Understand why what you do is valuable, and how to negotiate for more. If you worry that this job is the only way you'll pay the mortgage, how able are you to have difficult chats if the ethics go down the tube? Understand why you are valuable – not just here but everywhere.

10 Make sure every day contains one thing that you enjoy doing. (Tip: look for the things you are good at.)

"Son, we need to spend more quality time together. Stop by my office and fill out a job application."

Copyright 2003 by Randy Glasbergen. www.glasbergen.com

Whatever your view, work plays a big role in our lives, with the potential to create or destroy well-being. One indication of how important work is to us are the statistics on how we cope with unemployment; studies show that prolonged unemployment is one of the worst things to happen to a person, with a loss in self-esteem and aspiration on top of the financial difficulties.

Job security is a key part of our happiness at work. As individuals, we're quite keen on job security, but most organisations, certainly private sector ones, believe in workforce flexibility to meet the needs of a changing marketplace, and keep costs down. In practice this means no one has a job for life any more. But, perhaps controversially, I don't think that is a bad thing, as long as you can grow the skills to stay valuable. Why do I say that? Well, for one thing, jobs for life have a tendency to bore the life out of us anyway.

As a gorgeous, unique and gifted person (yes you), it wouldn't be the best thing for your learning and creative self to spend quiet years in an organisation where the jobs never change, where no one fails or gets fired and where the core activities stay the same. You'd have job security, but little challenge or stimulation. OK, if security ranked as your top priority for happiness, bingo. A win–win, provided that didn't sound too exciting. But happy?

Alternatively, you could work for a firm which constantly changes, grows, morphs, downsizes, outsources. A place where people come and go with remarkable speed, with lots of contractors or consultants for maximum flexibility, where the job is a rush to catch up with markets and customers who are highly demanding and in constant flux. Working there would probably contain a good amount of learning, creativity and pressure – but not feel at all secure. So if buzz and speed and pressure ranked as your top priority for happiness – bingo again. Though you'd probably be too busy to take a breath and ask "Am I happy?"

The quality of working life we demand has a great deal to do with our expectations about happiness at work, as I'll explain. If you expect work to be a place where you grow, learn and succeed, you'll be drawn to environments that encourage this. If you expect work to be a place where you get exploited, bored silly and leave owing them money, maybe you'll understandably want the least contact with the workplace possible. And not enjoy it.

To expand on the earlier quote by Abraham Lincoln: "Most people are about as happy in their work as they make their minds up to be." I'm not wishing to dismiss the unfair aspects of the employment market: real discrimination does exist and the market is, at best, amoral in how it treats "human resources". It just seems that some people seem able to find fulfilling, well-paid work, when others with similar skills and background find much less.

What's Your Happiness Plan?

Spend more time in the Far East and spend less time listening to Radio Four. The media in the UK pours a gentle blanket over independent thought, a morass of information and pre-digested newsak that informs on a global scale but with little useful to say about life on a human level.

Andrew, journalist

SO THE QUESTION IS, HOW TO DESIGN THE HAPPIEST VERSION OF THE JOB YOU CURRENTLY DO?

I'd like to suggest that if your starting point is that work can make you happy, you'll not only get through the least stimulating aspects, but you'll also discover wings to help you design a happier job. That's right. A Happiness Plan for work will lift your ambitions, talents and hopes to another level. This does need to take into account the grim nature of some things we're paid to do. I'm not going to be princess peachy here, I know scrubbing the floor in a pub isn't a cue for joy. Ploughing through your twentieth customer complaint of the day doesn't usually mean it either.

However, and quoting a source you may not have expected (Mary Poppins), sang: "In every job that must be done, there is an element of fun. You find the fun and snap! The job's a game…" And the evidence agrees – finding the part of any task that lets you enjoy talents and values will make it more enjoyable. So the question is, how to design the happiest version of the job you currently do? By the way, are you allowed to read a book that quotes Mary Poppins? You sure?

Say we did this properly, with clipboards and all, and ran a survey to ask your work colleagues to describe their levels of day-to-day happiness. What do you think we'd find out? Most people fulfilled, animated and lifted by their work? Not at all? Or too scared to say how they honestly view the situation because it might come back to them? And, if you don't mind my asking a personal question, what would your answer be?

I suspect that the question of happiness at work is also related to issues of unemployment and the whole job security question. Fear of losing our jobs often causes us to accept less than we could actually achieve. There are real financial demands; the mortgage payment, the cost of keeping a home stocked and ready to enjoy, not to mention the aspirational purchases, the holidays and special "treats". If you think about work in a certain way, the priority will be keeping that monthly salary safe, even if it means swallowing the day-to-day frustration. Happiness doesn't get onto the list of things to do today.

What I'd like to suggest is that this level of personal compromise, this sacrificial relationship you have with your job, is not only preventing your happiness – you know that. It is also blocking your chances of success and potential increase in earnings. Perhaps I should explain that. I believe that the instinct for happiness is akin to your sense of purpose, driven from the deepest part of your individual nature.

Are you ever aware that something is going on inside you, a movement of hopes and dreams? A feeling which is more than emotion? It feels ultra personal, yours alone. It isn't easy to describe, it's hard to get at. People sometimes refer to a "calling". Your big I want, your life's destiny, the thing you were born to do. A career energised with worthwhile purpose maybe?

Going back to the task at hand – designing the happiest version of the job you currently do – you'll find the Happiness Plan works in two parts. One – just like the rest of the Happiness Plan, is to start with understanding where you are now, then follow the ABC – to open yourself to more happiness.

Would that be a good idea? In my view, one important kind of happiness is the sense of fulfilment from challenging, stimulating work. Have you ever had a work situation where you had to draw on all your talent and knowledge to sort something out? You were part scared, part inspired, motivated. Work can be one way to find out who we are, and what is important to us. It might be worth a reminder of what Seligman calls the three levels of happiness:

- **The Pleasant Life:** Satisfying the visceral pleasures of the body such as having a glass of good wine, a hot bath or a walk in the park. Such pleasures are transitory and superficial and cannot produce true well-being but can make life enjoyable for a moment.
- **The Good Life:** Engaging in activity, often social in nature, which causes vigorous enjoyment through a challenge – take up Sunday football or try writing a book.
- **The Meaningful Life:** The highest level of sustained happiness comes when people can give a wider meaning to their lives. Helping others through politics, voluntary work or religion can help people to realise that there is something bigger and more important than themselves.

Seligman, from *Authentic Happiness*

So let's start your plan for more happiness at work. First of all, a quick sense check on your current levels of happiness at work. On the spectrum below, could you show where you are?

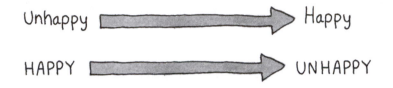

What's that? About a ……. out of 10?

Exercise When and where are you happiest – at work?

Close your eyes, think about it. Then write down whatever comes to mind here.

"I'm happiest at work when..."

Great. Where else? When else?...

There we are.

And now, is there anything you don't enjoy about your job?

"The following areas of my job are not making me happy just now..."

Should I have left more room on the page?

What does that make you think? Do you have as many good things to say about your job as bad things? Is this the same as you would have said a year ago? Asking yourself about happiness isn't always easy, but it is usually accurate.

So now, if you'd like to, we'll figure out a Happiness Plan for you and your work. Whatever that may be. Doesn't matter, the same rules apply.

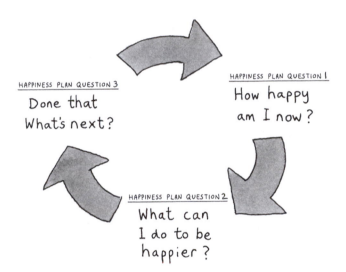

CAN YOU BE HAPPY IN A WAY THAT MAKES OTHERS HAPPY?

Relationships and love

According to an old Chinese saying, happiness is someone to love, something to do and something to hope for.

I was struck by the order of those. Someone to love is first and perhaps most important. Our need for romantic attachment, for love and intimacy is closely related to our survival. In fact, our perception of emotional support from another person can be the difference between life and death.

> When we feel loved by someone else, it has a measurable effect upon our health, as various studies have shown. It has a particularly positive effect upon – appropriately perhaps – the heart. High risk factors for heart problems such as cholesterol levels, diet, smoking, taking exercise and family history of heart disease have far less bearing on the outcome of heart disease than whether or not one feels emotionally supported by another person.
> *Joe Griffin and Ivan Tyrell.*[11]

What are the key sources of happiness with a relationship? This is a very subjective list, based on my research and some very personal experience!

- Touch – we have a survival-based need for physical contact
- Support and empathy – to be understood and held

[11] Griffin and Tyrell, *Human Givens: A New Approach to Emotional Health and Clear Thinking* (HG Publishing, 2003)

- The strength of the bond – from deep constant love to the mildest of attachments
- Attention – the quality and quantity of interaction
- Shared goals – as someone mentioned, love is not so much looking at each other, as both looking in the same direction
- Cooperation – the willingness to help and support.

In one study of married adults, 40 per cent called themselves "very happy" while only 23 per cent of those who had never married felt the same. This crosses all ethnic and national boundaries. It seems that marriage does more for our happiness than any amount of job satisfaction, more than our financial situation or community involvement.

The same story emerges from studies of people with depression. All other things being equal, married people are less depressed than never married people. In fact, several American studies have indicated that there's a very strong correlation between marital break-up and divorce rates and increases in depression.

ACCORDING TO AN OLD CHINESE SAYING, HAPPINESS IS SOMEONE TO LOVE, SOMETHING TO DO AND SOMETHING TO HOPE FOR.

This is clearly about the power of love, at the core of our emotions. What can we learn about love that can help grow the happiness in our closest relationships?

Apparently there are three kinds of love. The first kind is love of people who give us comfort, acceptance and help, people who bolster our confidence and guide us. The prototype for this kind of love is the love a child feels for a parent.

The second kind of love is for the people who depend on us for exactly the same things – the model for this being the love of a parent for their child.

The third kind of love is romantic love, the idealisation of another. We find no fault in this person. They have unique strengths and virtues, almost no shortcomings. We are in love. This definition of love (from a psychologist at Cornell University, Cindy Hazan) shows that marriage is unique as the arrangement that gives us all three kinds of love.

I am not sure if the first two kinds of love only apply to the parent–child relationship, or if we also share those dynamics with our romantic love.

Why have we evolved this strength of connectedness? It seems likely that the need to bond and stay close to one person is linked to our survival. As our children are born and stay defenceless for a fairly long period of time, supportive parents would make a big difference to the long term survival of the species. Think about that when next you consider the mountain of demands involved in raising a healthy, capable child! It's not just for you, it's for the whole race. Although at over 100 billion we humans seem to be doing just fine on survival!

So what does this good news about marriage mean for your Happiness Plan with your partner? And what does it mean if you are single? I realise the danger of what Bridget Jones called "smug marrieds" – all those years ago.

The content of your Happiness Plan depends on what kind of person you are. In terms of your closest relationships, this is directly linked to the quality of your early years as a child. Apparently each one of us has an emotional bias, which can be one of three things:

1 **We feel secure** – and have memories of available parental love, with warmth and affection. We are likely to feel confident and secure in our romantic attachments.

2 **We feel "avoidant"** – we remember our mothers (yes the research is specific) as being cold and far away. We don't trust others easily and prefer a more detached style of romance.

3 **We feel "anxious"** – we remember our fathers as being unfair (yes more specific research). We tend to feel insecure in our closest relationships, as if we need our loved one more than they need us.

What do you think about that? Does it seem true for you and people you know? Does it feel true in your closest relationship? And are you happy about it?

More to the point – what can you do?

ABC it?

If you are secure – could you run the ABC through again to find out how to be even happier?

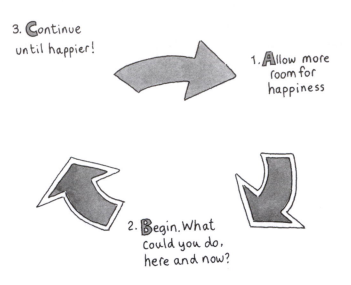

3. Continue until happier!

1. Allow more room for happiness

2. Begin. What could you do, here and now?

If you are avoidant – could the ABC exercise help?

Allow more room for happiness – via the risky business of trust, or becoming a little more tactile. Begin it – continue it?

If you are anxious – could the ABC exercise help once again?

Allow more room for happiness – via the risky business of letting go more. Not criticising? Begin it – continue it.

Happy ever after

Being in love is, in my view, the rocket fuel of personal happiness and there's no way to plan for it. Cue sighs. That sense of missing someone five minutes after you've said goodbye. Wanting to phone to describe the love you feel for them in great, urgent detail, just about stopping yourself. Waking up to waves of longing.

If all the happiness atoms of the world were combined into one moment, might that moment be when you get the first proper kiss with the love of your life?

Like so much else about happiness, scientists can tell you why something happens, and I would imagine being in love gets explained by our mammalian drive to ensure the survival of the gene pool, or some other equally poetic answer. But science has no way to predict or explain how it feels, or its importance to our well-being. Something extra happens. Back to the messy, unprogrammable human aspect of happiness. You can describe how hydrogen atoms combine with oxygen atoms in specific quantities to create water, with a tactile quality. Or you can tell me how it feels to swim in a cool sea on a hot day. And, also like happiness, falling in love doesn't tend to happen on cue, just because you've put the whole weekend aside. It happens when you are busy doing other things.

Growing up, I understood that finding the "one for you" and falling in love was the single most important thing I could do to "live happily ever after". Every magazine, every programme pointed to this source of indescribable joy. Young life was one long training programme in readiness for this union. What I didn't learn was that being in love brings as much pain as pleasure. You love and miss and long to kiss that soft sweet face and linger in their sweet embrace. Only they're watching telly. Or phoning mum. When they could come to bed.

Or you spend what feels like hundreds of years in a close relationship; outwardly loved up, tucked in. Inwardly, wildly insecure. Tip-toeing on eggshells forever.

Alternatively someone falls for you big time and hell needs to freeze over before you'd be alone with them. You don't notice this until they give a tearful or confrontational late night update. Ah. Sorry. Don't go to the same pub for a while. Feel guilty.

Or you're both already taken, but have moved beyond the just good friends stage. There's a little hop, skip and a jump going on when you're due to see them later. And you meet up every three months rather than every three days. You talk work, flirt – but stay sensible and chaste for the sake of key domestic stakeholders. You do, however, notice the similarity between the word chaste and the word waste.

The things that make us happiest are the things that also bring the greatest pain. Not sure this has helped at all, actually. I suppose the role of expert adviser just slipped away from me again …

I wonder – do any of these "happy ever afters" ring a bell for you? How would you describe your closest relationship just now? In good shape? Bit one-sided? Agony? Any Happiness Plan has to have the love plumbed in. The following pages might be able to give you some way to investigate.

Best of Both – A happiness win-win for lovers

OK. You know the Happiness Plan theory that happiness is usually a win–win. Did I mention that? Well, this is to find out how that's working in your love life. The goal here is to identify more ways to be happy in your relationship. You can add the detail below.

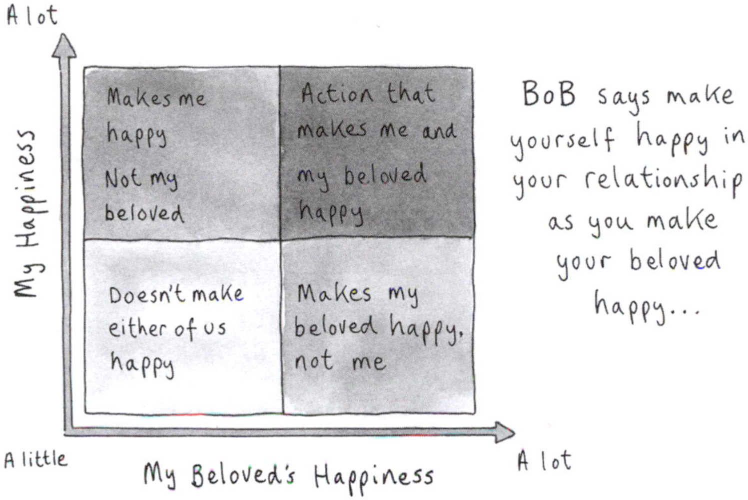
A lot
My Happiness
Makes me happy Not my beloved
Action that makes me and my beloved happy
Doesn't make either of us happy
Makes my beloved happy, not me
A little
My Beloved's Happiness
A lot
BoB says make yourself happy in your relationship as you make your beloved happy...

Exercise What builds happiness in your relationship?

What are the things that make neither of you happy?...

____

____

____

____

What are the things that wind you both up, that you'd both like to sort out?...

What are the things that make you happy, but not the one you love?...

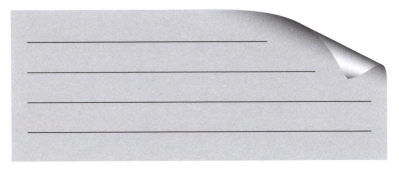

What makes your beloved happy, while driving you to distraction?...

What makes you both happy?...

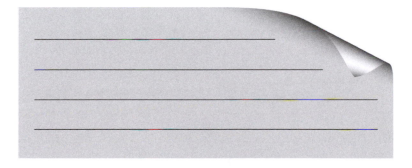

Out of these, what small action could you take (together as well as independently), to make a difference?...

I asked two people I know (not well, couldn't do this with my close friends for some reason) and this is how it worked for them.

Part 1. My Happiness - Siobhan

A four-quadrant grid with vertical axis labelled "My Happiness - Siobhan":

Makes me happy, Not my beloved "Seeing my family more often than we'd planned!" "The cats"	Action that makes me and my beloved happy "Going to the cinema" "Cooking a really nice meal at home"
Doesn't make either of us happy "Rows that start when we're both tired. We can't seem to help ourselves"	Makes my beloved happy, not me "Listening to his work problems, offering advice" "Curry"

The Happiness Plan for Siobhan would be what? Well, first of all for her and Steve to compare their Best of Both maps.

The question that springs to my mind is this. How do we make the most of whatever our natural romantic inclination might be? Is there a way to use the ABC way of thinking in our closest relationships to strengthen and improve the quality of these relationships?

Happier communities

Happiness has a biological rationale. It evolved as a strategy for human survival – and key to that is our sense of connectedness to others.

It might be worth a little history to show why human happiness is so dependent on our connectedness to others. About 35,000 years ago, give or take a few months, human beings started to evolve new mental skills. We changed from being purely reactive (uh oh, lion, run) to thinking in a more abstract way about our environment (aha, deer, create new weapon, use spear).

We started to access imagination, daydreams and plans, then used that extra thought capacity to gain advantage, specifically in hunting methods. The cave art of Lascaux in France seems to be one example – human beings depicting a future hunt, with prey shown in colour and accuracy. This capacity to develop imagination and harness the power of dreams probably drove the next evolutionary stage, about 10,000 years ago. Day-dreaming humans changed from being nomadic hunter/gatherers to settled farmers, domesticating and breeding previously wild animals, cultivating crops, learning about irrigation, food storage and inventing the motorbike. No, hang on, that came a little later.

This shift from hunting to farming was a huge evolutionary leap. We started to organise for future seasons, to co-operate with others, to create communal as well as purely selfish benefits.

The new thinking would have been accompanied by a suite of new emotions, designed to reinforce human bonds. We became more able to empathise, connect, build close communities with shared benefits. The farming community which depended on everyone at harvest time would only have succeeded if everyone in that community felt enough incentive. Those communities would not have thrived with constant separation and aggression. "He needs our help with the grain, but he's such a pain no one's going to bother. Shame, looks like no bread this winter." No. We've grown as loving, caring communities for some very practical reasons. We've carried on, much the same for about 21 centuries, growing our basic communities into cities, using our imagination and dreams to conjure up – well – a stunningly complex reality.

But where did the evolution of human happiness fit into all that? And has the pace of change separated us from the earth and the need for a co-operative society?

We've created a society geared to personal, sealed-away pleasure with individualised toys, music, homes, communities. The "on-demand" media revolution means you don't even have to watch telly en famille any more – I am starting to wonder if the extended family belongs in anthropology museums. I suppose the research on community life – particularly the higher levels of perceived happiness in communities where trust and collaboration score highly – could lead to some questions. As a society, what kind of vision for shared happiness are we trying to create? Do we have, for example:

- A desire to ensure all children are supported to learn, and become successful adults?
- A desire to involve and integrate newer immigrants to our society?
- A belief that good health and happiness can be enjoyed by everyone, not just those with a particular background or income bracket?
- A desire to do more than work, spend and sleep?

CLOSED DOWN, SHUT OUT. THE IPOD GENERATION

On the train home this evening, a particularly handsome young man sat opposite me, reading, with his earphones plugged in. He got up to leave the train, at exactly the same time as a particularly beautiful young woman and they smiled awkwardly. Both kept in earphones, both looked down or away, back into the enjoyment of their own individual music. The moment, if there ever was one, had passed. Both smiled at each other as they got off.

Now, call me old-fashioned, but wouldn't the absence of iPods make a difference in those moments? Rather than being closed down, with all human contact shut out, accidental meetings could turn into something. Or am I just being an old romantic?

Opened up, welcomed in

The opposite of closed down, shut out. OK, not going to happen in some more culturally reserved places, but imagine. Imagine if the journey sometimes meant an interesting conversation. Or a joke. Or just a shared observation. The hermetically sealed space – particularly of the under-25s – seems to preclude random contact. Is that always for the best?

Perhaps there is room for a gentle optimism about the role of happiness in transforming society. Earlier on I wrote about being a pro-person, rather than an anti-person. We can talk for a long time about inequalities, about the rise of poverty-related illnesses, and about the widening gap betweeen rich and poor.

My suggestion is that if we consider the foundations that need to be in place for health, happiness and well-being, we could have another route to solving the biggest social ills of our day. We could just ask – how does this child go from where he or she is now (let's say under-performing at school because of a lack of parental support, or nutrition, or self-belief) to a happier life?

We could use the Happiness Plan to offer a flexible structure to think through the changes needed to create more happiness in that child's life. It is hard to see how a society that ignores poverty can be a happier society, and yet many of us feel over-whelmed by the injustice around us. What can be done?

Perhaps the most powerful part of the Happiness Plan, when it comes to making a difference in the world, would be this. **Your contribution level equals your fulfilment level**. By helping others achieve their goals, you create a better outcome for them as well as a sense of pride and personal fulfilment within yourself. How many times do you give yourself the chance to do that? Could be an idea to up the average.

Maybe there has never been a better time to re-evaluate our priorities as a society, because something positive seems to be going on. There is a gentle movement away from excessive and conspicuous consumption, from less green to more green lifestyles, from business that doesn't care to business that has to care. These gentle shifts are happening because the way we think is changing.

At a personal level, we are becoming less content at the prospect of sleepwalking through another fifty years at work, paying bills, struggling on without considering personal well-being or happiness. I suggest that the Happiness Plan could mark a turning point in your life, where your focus widens to include more time for yourself, more space for love in your relationships, more wakefulness about your health and well-being. Doing this will, I promise, add the right level of perspective and energy to do even better at your work; when we know that the long day ahead is a choice, our personal motivation and desire to enjoy goes up a level. Are you ready to take that step – to live a happier life?

The future of happiness

Carrying on from that idea that happiness is part of a more positive social vision, here are five trends for the future. You heard them here first!

1 Social offsetting: being good (to be happy)

(Something like carbon offsetting, only now with social exclusion.)

Example: The investment banker who receives a £1 million Xmas bonus and chooses to spend £1,000 to socially offset their Ferrari. They offset using a socially useful agency, a social enterprise or charity. An example of that agency would be Magic Breakfast, the award-winning charity delivering free breakfast food to the (1 in 4) London primary schoolchildren who arrive too hungry to learn.

Social offsetting will grow alongside large-scale philanthropy, simply because richer individuals will want to feel better about their contribution, and legacy. Just as organisations want to claim their green or social credentials, those in the richest sector will want to retain their connected humanity through actions that offset a small (very small) proportion of their wealth. There is only so much kudos with wealth, particularly in the age of billionaire expansion. There is, however, still mileage in being a generous, thoughtful and socially impactful person. This is where social offsetting will grow. *Have you started social offsetting yet?*

2 Happiness coaching becomes big business

A few years ago the desire to live a healthier life was a minority interest. I predict that the healthy-eating gurus will be joined, if not superseded by, a range of happiness coaches. The advice will cover: "Being happier while you raise your kids"; "Being happier while you start your first enterprise". There'll be conferences on "Happiness chemistry in relationships", how to create the happier workplace; how to raise happier children. Yes I know, this may seem far-fetched. But so did intrusive food advice ten years ago and guess what? Today I've got less junk food in my cupboard and I bet you do too.

3 Happiness for performance: brain food and laughter classes

My guess is that popular science will seek to maximise the effectiveness of pleasure centres of your brain, through mood-boosting food, a range of bad science vitamin supplements and lifestyle choice. If we aim to maximise the career length and productiveness of our fewer workers, then being fit, in terms of capacity to relax and recharge, will become essential.

The system that burned people out, made them want to down-shift/size/tools and start an organic farm, will eventually seem as archaic as the bowler-hats on city bankers heading to desks in English-owned banks. It will be replaced by a system that says performance requires health and well-being, specifically individual quality of life, sense of purpose and enough time for pleasure. Mind gyms, with meditation, groups listening to laughter tracks, and NLP coaching will become almost as common as body gyms. Graduate entrants will learn that mental agility, work focus and effort need to be balanced with mental restfulness and laughter. Does that sound good or bad? I've no doubt that the largest firms in the global economy will hardwire newest trends from positive psychology to increase profits. But that doesn't mean that we, as individuals, can't reap the benefits as well, or even in advance.

The corporate workplace, for example, is capable of incredible adaptation to retain resources and therefore market advantage. Remember when the man wasn't even considered a parent? Wifey did everything child-wise, and housework was a particular blessing in her life. She did tend to lose out on her career, because that was considered normal and right. Now, somehow, paternity leave is considered acceptable and planned for, even in the most corporate setting. Why? Because this nod to family happiness is seen as a right, from being a negotiated special arrangement. Employee happiness will increasingly be seen in the same light, using the same system of "most valuable employees first". And perhaps, one day, wifey won't do all the housework as well.

The trend is going to hit in another significant area. I think the urge for self-actualisation is going to grow as more of us seek a sense of identity and personal moral purpose, outside of conspicuous consumption. Having stuff, and doing busy but cool things is not giving us the spiritual nutrition we need, and this junk diet is having a pretty uncool effect on our well-being. But there's evidence we're waking up to the problem. There is an astonishing increase in the volume of titles on authenticity, meaning, finding the answer to "Who am I?"

4 Thrift, green mainstream and local reconnection

In some ways, yes I am a cheerleader for the finding of purpose in life, partly because it seems a waste to spend too many decades in gentle aimlessness when it could be really enjoyable. And partly because life is, in my view, that big bit better when we know more about ourselves and our capacity for great things. One example of this came recently in the charity I work with. Magic Breakfast delivers free, healthy food to primary schools where children arrive too hungry to learn. We've got a social enterprise arm to help fund, but sadly we still get more schools applying for urgent support than we can reach with immediate food deliveries. About a year ago a very gentle young man, David, offered to help raise funds for us. He works as a model, leads a pretty cool life by all accounts, but he wanted to offer his time and effort for free. Why? He said that "I go to far too many champagne receptions, I want to feel more sense of moral purpose and direction". We've so far been able to open three primary school breakfast clubs because of David's help.

5 Getting a purpose check alongside the health check

Now clearly everyone has a different set of needs, so it may be that you feel little or no need to find work with purpose, no hankering for a more meaningful challenge. The most important thing is to consider which kind of happiness you are looking for – to be specific. If your whole life is spent caring for someone, the Happiness Plan may well require an increase in time with popcorn at the multiplex and no big thinking.

Whatever your happiness focus, this is just my view on the next trend to help you get your blues on the mend and send a nice message to the person watching you read this book. Everything is going to be fine, because in this big new century we started using green fuel, eating less poison and realising that lightening up is a priority for the masses.

Seeing trends is part of becoming valuable as well as understanding who you are and what is most important to you. More future stuff will be:

- Barter/thrift/craft
- *Second Life*, social networking technology as the new brand frontier
- Social enterprise embeds, CEOs call themselves social entrepreneurs
- Coastal cool communities
- Urban Raleigh – students and mid-life gap year work in inner cities at home to reduce their carbon prints and become, like, reconnected locally
- Micro-lending and credit unions to tackle debt

- Mobile phone economy
- Pre-pay credit
- Individualised economy vs. social networks e.g. pooled childcare, shopping and cars

If this is where society might be heading, what are you going to do to consider your future happiness needs? A happiness forecast? Surely, becoming much warmer later....

While we're on the subject of the future, let's come back to an important one. Yours.

Exercise A letter from my (happier) future self

This is a letter, written by you from your life in one year's time. You are writing to the person you are today, one year earlier.

By jumping forward one year, you can imagine yourself in a better place, perhaps able to see your life from a different viewpoint.

Please imagine it is one year exactly from today, and you are writing a letter to the person you are, right here today. Try it!

Dearest

I am writing this letter to you, to let you know how things worked out during the past 12 months. As I look at my life, right now, the things I am most happy about are as follows (write here the areas of your life you expect to be going well in that future time).

I am most happy about…

The things I'm still working on are …

Looking back over the past 12 months, I am really pleased about the changes I was able to make.

In my work...

In my personal life...

In other ways...

I have thought about how I was able to make these changes, and I see that I took some small steps along the way, and maybe some bigger ones too. These are the steps which I think helped me make those changes…

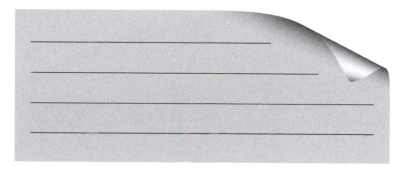

The baby steps I remember were…

The bigger steps I remember were…

And I am glad I took action over the year, because I realise that it was my responsibility to create a Happiness Plan, and improve life for myself. I feel better! In terms of timescales, it was important to take some action on a regular basis. Looking back, during the first six months, this is what I decided to do.

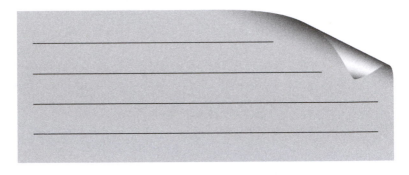

And I decided to follow with...

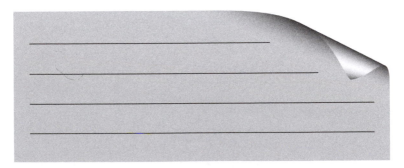

Most recently, I have taken the following action...

I can see, looking back at how I was, I had some fears and hopes. So I have some advice to you, the person I was back then. My advice is this...

With love,

How do you plan to make yourself happy in the future?

"Continue to work on the 'balance' between a happy and productive work life and an enjoyable home/social life. I am a firm believer in having interests (especially sporting interests) outside work that enable time for contemplation and relaxation as well as enjoyment."
Mark Powell, Chief Architect, Zurich Financial Services

Things do not change;
we change.

Henry James Thoreau

SOME HAPPINESS PLAN EXAMPLES

06

The Happiness Plan steps

STEP 1	Decide to be happier (the ABC approach)
STEP 2	Understand happiness
STEP 3	Create a personal Happiness Plan
STEP 4	Unlearn unhappiness
STEP 5	Our plan. Make others happy
STEP 6	**Some Happiness Plan examples**
STEP 7	Put your plan into action

Happiness planning for four major life areas

You might wonder at that. Surely no one but you can create your Happiness Plan? Yep, that is true. But wouldn't it be a good idea to know the ways that your Happiness Plan could be of service, if you were faced with some big decisions, such as leaving your job?

Over many years of working on change and leadership, I've noticed that the same questions get asked time and time again, and are very often directed towards the same highly prized outcomes. Such as the four following examples.

1 **Career fulfilment.** How can I tell if my job will enable me to live a purposeful, successful life? Specifically, how do I negotiate my role, so it includes more of what I enjoy and am good at?

2 **Time.** How can I have more time for things other than work? Preferably without penury! Specifically – how do I manage to bag a four-day week?

3 **Relationships.** How can I improve my closest, most loving relationships? Specifically, how do we create a closer bond, so we can get through the hard times?

4 **Financial control.** How can I earn enough to do more than just work to pay bills? Specifically, to control my finances?

So this section considers how the ideas from your Happiness Plan can be used to answer some of those questions. The way to do this is obviously not generic, or even similar, from one person to another. Every answer is unique, but how you get to the answer may be through the same sort of approach, using questions and exercises to find your own answers.

On all of these, the core Happiness Plan principles apply:

- **Your happiness depends on you**
  - Your capacity for perspective – being able to assess your current state,
  - Your action to improve the situation and,
  - Having a sense of personal responsibility for ongoing improvements.
- **Harness the power of your mental "space between".** What messages are playing there right now? Please remember that your thoughts create your life. What's in your head

right now is the script for what happens tomorrow – so become more aware of your inner supporter, or inner nag.

■ **Happiness can become your underlying intention, supporting everything you do.** This is more likely to create happiness habits or routines. The habit of checking to make sure you are not becoming overloaded at work, or making sure you do something really enjoyable every week.

So, let's consider these questions in turn, using the Happiness Plan.

First of all – the small, minor question of work. Let's assume for the moment that it is going pretty well, but could be better. And you'd appreciate any indication of your life's purpose.

Ready-made Happiness Plan for a more fulfilling career

"Desired outcome: To feel that my work is purposeful, stimulating – and right for me."

It is certainly possible to negotiate for more fulfilment. In my experience it comes with the following proviso. In terms of your career, personal fulfilment is closely linked to your personal contribution. Roughly speaking, this means that the more you expect fulfilment as part of the package, the less likely it is to appear. The more you understand the needs of those around you, and take care to offer your time and effort, the more likely you are to feel fulfilled.

> This is the true joy in life, the being used for a purpose recognised by yourself as a mighty one; the being thoroughly worn out before you are thrown on the scrap heap; there being a force of Nature, instead of a feverish selfish little clod of ailments and grievances complaining that the world will not devote itself to making you happy.
>
> George Bernard Shaw

Using your Happiness Plan will help you make better career decisions even if you don't know the first move to your life's purpose. Even if all you feel is "there should be more to life". How can it do this? By steering by what is most important to you. And we can start to find that out with these questions.

Quiz Do your values align with those at work?

1 Broadly, do you identify with the objectives of your organisation (or where you work if that isn't the right description)?

- Yes
- No
- Not sure
- Don't know what the objectives of my organisation are.

2 Do the values of the organisation feel right to you: do you have similar personal values? Values could be, for example, honesty, putting customers first, showing respect to all employees, being risk takers. (NB The values might be shown somewhere on the website, sometimes hidden under governance, or mission, rather strangely.) Although it is much better if they are shown in the day-to-day behaviour of those who run the place.

So, going back to the question, do you share the values of your workplace?

- Yes
- No
- Not sure
- Don't know what they are.

3 Would you say you feel trusted by your boss and your colleagues? For example, do they allow you to interpret your role with some individuality? How much slack are you cut? Are you known as reliable?

- Yes
- No
- Not sure.

4 Do you generally trust those around you? Likewise, do you believe that they will honour promises, do things when they say they will? Do you believe in them?

- Yes
- No
- Not sure.

So what are your answers showing up to now?

- If mostly "yes", then perhaps a happy fit with the firm.
- If mostly no, perhaps a firm uh-oh to the firm.
- If you have mostly "not sure", perhaps this shows that you are firmly undecided?

Glad we were able to firm that up. The next few questions look at your current levels of engagement and fulfilment at work.

5 When and where are you happiest at work?

"I'm happiest at work when ..."

6 With a bit of negotiation, would it be possible to do more of that thing that makes you happiest at work, in a way that would make a difference to your customers (or users, or clients – whoever needs you to do something to help them)? External feedback from those you support will make the case – or not. What do you think – is it possible?

- Yes
- No
- Not sure.

7 Overall, how happy are you with your current work? (Put a mark on the spectrum below.)

Unhappy ➡ Happy

HAPPY ➡ UNHAPPY

8 If you were to be given a magic wand, which three things would you want to change about work, so that it felt more appealing and stimulating?

■ First thing...

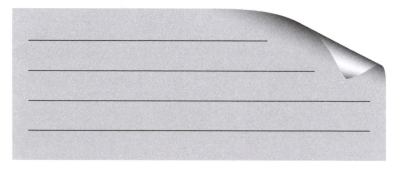

_____

_____

_____

_____

■ Second thing...

_____

_____

_____

_____

■ Third thing...

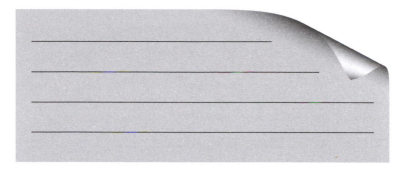

9 What would be the biggest difference, if each one of those changes were to happen?

10 Finally, what has this set of questions brought to light?

How well do you fit with your current workplace, in terms of agreeing with the broad objectives and values?

How are the trust levels?

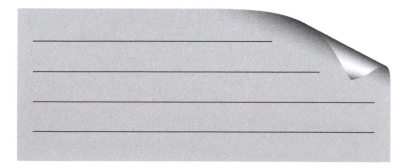

Do you enjoy your work – could you find lots of things that make you happy (or did 6pm Friday spring to mind?)

What do you want to change – and why?

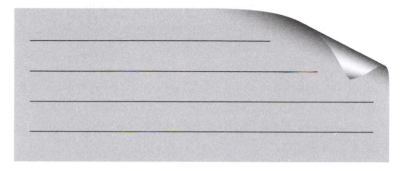

In an earlier book (*Soultrader*, Momentum 2002) I suggested that there is only one decision to take at any point in your career. That question is:

Should I stay, or should I go? Yes, a question just begging to be sung.

So you decided:

"I'm going to stay."

Or

"I'm going to leave."

Which was it again? No need to sing ... thanks.

The decision to stay or leave then begs another question. You've decided to...

1 **Stay and do nothing**. Mindset = I am in transition, out of here, ready to take action when the time is right. I'm looking for another job and will leave when I find it.

Or

2 **Stay and negotiate**. Work out what needs to improve in order for you to feel happy, fulfilled and successful. Decide to make improvements, negotiate for more happiness and stay.

Or

3 **Leave for a new but similar job**. Move job, and stay in the same field to be closer to what feels like your life purpose.

Or

4 **Leave for something completely different**. Create something completely different for yourself.

IN OUR CAREERS, WE GET WHAT WE THINK WE'LL GET. WHAT DO YOU THINK YOU DESERVE?

That's all I'm going to cover on the off-the-shelf Happiness Plan for more career fulfilment. The next stage is to consider whether the time for action is now, or if you need to ask friends, family, colleagues for their opinion and work things out a bit more clearly. Keep steering by your happiness and remember the fulfilment/contribution link. It will work out.

I am going to combine the next two from the list at the start of the chapter – because in my experience the search for more time, such as the the Holy Grail of a four-day week, is often linked to a desire to meet the needs of loved ones. Perhaps it's being available for a dependant – whether that is caring for an elderly parent, or wanting to see your youngest take their first step. So the Happiness Plan is going to be put to work to consider how to get a four-day week, so you can have more time for the ones you love.

Managing time: The four-day week Happiness Plan

How can I have more time for things other than work? Preferably without penury! Specifically – how do I manage to bag a four-day week?

There are two things to check before we start:

1 Would more time at home, away from work, make you happier?
2 Would the people you plan to spend more time with be happier if you did?

Sorry if that sounds a bit odd – it's just that flawed assumptions can cause an awful lot of confusion. So, you will be happier and they will be happier. Just thought I'd check.

CAN YOU MAKE HAPPINESS A HABIT?

Core principles

The negotiation that you may need to have with your employer to gain a four-day week is based on a number of major factors. We'll take a look at these from your side, and from their side. From your side, key factors influencing the negotiation include:

- Your value to the organisation – how much do they need your unique skills, know-how and expertise? What are you worth to the organisation – both now and in the future?
- The urgency of your request. If your dependant is not well, for example, and needs a variety of carers.
- Your standing at work. No, not a capacity to lurk in corridors! By this I mean your reputation, depth of professional relationships and potential.
- Your ability to delegate and manage the workload in four days.
- Your negotiation skills. Do you know how to, or will it be torture to ask?
- Research and inside knowledge. Your awareness of any similar requests and results within the organisation, or comparable organisations. If Sean from Marketing was allowed a four-day week to do an MBA, does that mean they are more or less likely to grant your request?

From your employer's side, key factors might be:

- Your capacity to meet most of the requirements of the job in four days.
- Your worth – are you a star performer to keep at almost any cost? Or not?

- The adverse effect of refusal on your morale particularly in a hot employment market when you may leave for a more flexible employment offer.
- The precedent it might set – is this a simple one-off, or the opening of floodgates? This is most keenly felt in terms of impact on other employees, either in terms of increased workload or the sense that others are left behind in less favourable working arrangements.
- The pay and benefit discussion – will this request be for fewer hours, meaning less pay, or is there an expectation of four longer working days?
- Awareness of current trends and the right thing to do as a good employer, within the requirements of maintaining performance.

The plan. Remember that lasting happiness is a win–win. Your employer will be as happy as you are at the end of this process, or else something will go wrong later on.

Negotiation for a four-day week: the Happiness Plan principles

1 Your happiness depends on you.

So, in this case, you'll need to do the research to make the best possible case, and negotiate with your employer. Also, you'll be responsible for making sure the workload is managed, or delegated appropriately. And you will need to have a response for a refusal, or if they say yes but with conditions you cannot accept. Are you ready? How can you get your case together?

2 Harness the power of your mental "space between". What messages are playing there right now? Please remember that your thoughts create your life. What's in your head right now is the script for what happens tomorrow – so become more aware of your inner supporter, or inner nag.

Perhaps the thoughts playing in your "space between" say you have no chance of getting a four-day week. What would that underlying message do for your application? Or perhaps you're going to create a conflict – if they don't let you have a four-day week, after all you've done for them, etc. etc. What would be the most encouraging, supporting thoughts for this situation?

3 Happiness can become your underlying intention, supporting everything you do. This is more likely to create happiness habits or routines. The habit of checking to make sure you are not becoming overloaded at work, or making sure you do something really enjoyable every week.

You can imagine a situation where work is going really well at four days a week, with regular updates with your boss to make sure all is well. The routine you have installed is better feedback between your team and customers, and between you and your boss – so even if you spend less time at work, you are able to be better prepared and spend less time firefighting. And your home life and health are so much better now you have that extra day. You've seen a way to be happier and made it happen. Congratulations!

Set the intention

Take the brakes off; play these messages in your space between

I deserve to be happy right now.

Not later when....

It's OK to have money. It's OK to have enough time.

Gently...

...on the accelerator; play these messages to move your happiness forward

What makes me happy in my work right now?

What makes me happy and also makes my customers happy?

How can I do more of that so that I become more valuable to my employer?

So how are you going to do it?

By taking the employer's viewpoint, and answering their needs one by one. We listed the employer's key criteria a little earlier. Let's look at each of these in more detail.

Your capacity to meet most of the requirements of the job in four days

What is the workload – realistically? Look at your objectives (if you have them) and consider those first. Then think of all the extra duties you have. You might be working day number five just on the unseen extras, like the ad hoc reports for your boss, or the extra time you choose to spend mentoring the younger members of your team. Then there is the time-wasting, procrastination, useless meetings and wasted travel to consider. That all adds up!

Can you show that you will be able to do the job in four days? Does this require delegation or extra resource to be bought in? Answer this question from your employer's viewpoint first.

Your worth – are you a star performer to keep at almost any cost?

How can you tell your real worth? You know how much you get paid. But say you had to describe why the firm pays your salary, in terms of economic benefit? Or if you were asked to give a day rate for your work as a contractor – what would you say? In some ways this is a very good question to ask, regardless of your four-day week adventure.

Exercise My worth in the marketplace – a ready reckoner

	Is this a good description of my current employment situation?	Answer yes or no
1	If I left, my employer would have to quickly fill my position.	
2	The advert would need to be supplemented with an expensive search via a specialist agency to find candidates with the same skills as me.	
3	If I were to leave, it is likely that the firm would lose revenue in the short term, because of my contribution.	
4	My qualifications, professional apprenticeship and career achievements mean that I am reasonably secure in my role.	
5	The people I deal with every day are valued customers or suppliers. My relationship with them has taken a long time to establish.	
6	I am seen as a thought leader here, keeping other colleagues aware of the most important developments in the field.	
7	If we had to reduce the numbers of people employed here, I am sure someone would make sure I was retained.	
8	I am asked for my professional opinion by the trade press.	

	Is this a good description of my current employment situation?	Answer yes or no
9	I speak at conferences and have written articles on my specialist subject.	
10	I receive the best professional development and HR support possible.	
11	My experience is unique in the firm, I often help and mentor others.	
12	If I wanted to, it is likely that I could seek promotion to the highest level of the firm.	
13	If I wanted to, I would be able to leave and be re-employed on a contract to do what I do now, probably at a much higher salary (but no pension or holiday).	
14	I am aware of the market value (in terms of freelance rates) for my peers.	
15	My network is such that I would easily get freelance work at a good day rate, doing what I do now.	
16	If I wanted to, I could start a consultancy practice, doing what I do here with a wider variety of organisations.	

How many times did you answer yes? Clearly the more the better, in terms of your awareness of your market worth, as well as your capacity to negotiate with your current employer. The ready reckoner also points out some of the stages of professional recognition that are often (but not always) tied to worth. In some professions such as academia, thought leadership, professional speaking and writing are almost part of the job, and won't automatically ensure a higher market rate – but may lead to greater security of tenure. In others, such as technology or human resources, industry profile can lead to higher earnings.

Of course, the key here is to be able to make the most of your skills and experience, so that when that four-day week conversation begins, your employer is willing to negotiate because you are valuable. But it could go two ways, even if you can be confident on value. If you are very valuable, the employer might want all your available time. However, they won't want to upset you. Which brings me to the next area you need to negotiate.

The adverse effect of refusal on your morale

What would you do if they said no? Accept and withdraw? Offer a second bid? The good employer would be keen to make sure you didn't feel badly treated and so consider leaving. So what would your Happiness Plan suggest? Probably that you should focus on the part of the job you did enjoy, and work out how to return with a new offer or suggestion in the near future.

BUILD THE CASE FOR YOUR IDEAL JOB, BASED ON THE VALUE YOU ADD, PLUS YOUR PERSONAL HAPPINESS PLAN.

The precedent it might set – is this a simple one-off, or the opening of floodgates?

This is most keenly felt in terms of impact on other employees, either in terms of increased workload or the sense that others are left behind in less favourable working arrangements.

This isn't something you'll have a great deal of control over. However, you need to be aware of their thinking. In a small organisation this is clearly more manageable than in a global multinational where the effects of one decision could cause serious repercussions. Be aware, though, of the argument used in any similar cases. Use the web and trade press to find out if your competitors or suppliers have a four-day week rule for employees like you. And ask your friends – how does their employer deal with this request?

The pay and benefit discussion – will this request be for fewer hours, meaning less pay, or is there an expectation of four longer working days?

This is likely to be crucial – what is most important to your happiness? If you have to retain the income, you'll need to prove five goes into four, realistically. So be really clear on what you can afford to do before they ask the question. If you don't need to retain your full salary, are you sure and have you thought it through?

Your Happiness Plan will ask you to prioritise. Does your homelife happiness depend more on time, or the peace of mind from financial security? Do you know the exact changes to your income if you do move to a four-day salary from five?

Whatever your personal requirement, make sure that partners and any other dependencies share your view!

Awareness of current trends and the right thing to do as a good employer

This is in your favour as an employee. There is no doubt that more employers are open to paternity leave, sabbaticals, study leave and, provided there is no detrimental effect on performance, four-day week arrangements. So be there with your evidence showing how a happier workforce is a motivated workforce. And show them the data in your industry if possible.

Financial control – a Happiness Plan

How can I earn enough to do more than just work to pay bills? Specifically, to control my finances?

We talked earlier about Hedonic adaptation, that downright catchy term to describe how we quickly get used to each new increase in living standards, and decide we need an upgrade. Any off-the-shelf plan has to be mindful of this, and there are three (fairly controversial) parts to consider.

1 Look at what you've already got – and appreciate the happiness that could already be there. Still under warranty, unpaid for.

2 Ask yourself what the "new must have" will give your life – what is the essence of the improvement? If you want some more green space in your life, more time with nature,

perhaps a walk in the park at lunchtime could do it for you. You may not need the rural retreat after all.

3 Find out if financial control is linked to your "space between" – the inner voice that suggests you are an inadequate person without possession x or y. Or which tells you (rather perversely) that you are equally inadequate if you do have possession x or y.

I'm not going to talk about how you earn more money in this section; that was, I hope, covered in the question on how to negotiate a four-day week.

In this final "off-the-shelf" Happiness Plan, perhaps we could consider why your financial controls might be located on the inside, in your thoughts and behaviours, rather than outside, with your bank or your boss or your credit card company.

Let's consider the first two of those.

1 Look at what you've already got, before getting a new one

Clearly a mad idea, as the new one will be better than the old one, and all the really cool people know that. But if you knew that new was just a very temporary – almost momentary high – would you still be so keen? In our rush to acquire, be seen with, consume, we just seem to have a shorter and shorter span of enjoyment.

Take this example – this weekend's latest brush with built-in obsolescence. My mobile phone is out of warranty (I got it a year ago). There have been five new upgrade handsets in the meantime, and by the way, all the cables and memory cards have changed, so you need new everything. OK? Or can I just keep this perfectly good one. Er – OK. But you could upgrade today. And buy all new cards, cables and not even transfer all the data without taking a week off work to read the manual. That's right madam. Shall I get the box for you? I know that it risks deep un-coolness to have an old phone. But I am willing to have the 2008 handset until 2009. Call me crazy.

2 Ask yourself what the "new must have" will give your life – what is the essence of the improvement?

Are you sure you need to buy that something, when all sorts of magnificent happiness is there, free, waiting for you to claim it?

The following is the short story of someone who chose to be happy now. Not later. In some ways, this is the final part of the story.

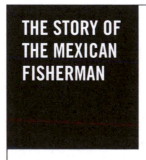

THE STORY OF THE MEXICAN FISHERMAN

An American investment banker was at the pier of a small coastal Mexican village when a small boat with just one fisherman docked. Inside the small boat were several large yellowfin tuna. The American complimented the Mexican on the quality of his fish and asked how long it took to catch them. The Mexican replied, "Only a little while."

The American then asked why didn't he stay out longer and catch more fish?

The Mexican said he had enough to support his family's immediate needs. The American then asked, "But what do you do with the rest of your time?" The Mexican fisherman said, "I sleep late, fish a little, play with my children, take siestas with my wife, Maria, stroll into the village each evening where I sip wine, and play guitar with my amigos. I have a full and busy life."

The American scoffed, "I am a Harvard MBA and could help you. You should spend more time fishing and with the proceeds, buy a bigger boat. With the proceeds from the bigger boat, you could buy several boats, eventually you would have a fleet of fishing boats. Instead of selling your catch to a middleman, you would sell directly to the processor, eventually opening your own cannery. You would control the product, processing, and distribution. You would need to leave this small coastal fishing village and move to Mexico City, then LA and eventually New York City, where you will run your expanding enterprise."

The Mexican fisherman asked, "But, how long will all this take?" To which the American replied, "15–20 years."

But what then?" asked the Mexican.

The American laughed and said, "That's the best part. When the time is right you would announce an IPO and sell your company stock to the public and become very rich, you would make millions!" "Millions – then what?"

The American said, "Then you would retire. Move to a small coastal fishing village where you would sleep late, fish a little, play with your kids, take siestas with your wife, stroll to the village in the evenings where you could sip wine and play your guitar with your amigos."

Last thoughts. Happiness is best kept simple

I really liked that story when I first read it, in the middle of a too busy, stress-filled life a few years ago, and it gave me reason to think. I hope it gives something of the essence of the Happiness Plan. The essence, I hope, can be summarised like this.

Happiness isn't complicated. It's not a luxury, a rare or precious or unattainable prize. It is in your DNA to be happy and enjoy life, just as much as to work hard and frown convincingly. But how many of us do the equivalent of "stroll to the village in the evenings where you could sip wine and play your guitar with your amigos"?

Here's an easy thing to try. Today, for example, you could have a mull on what's going well in your life, focus on one of those things, feel warmed and a little cheery round the edges. Then get on the phone and plan something nice for this evening.

Or, you could do the opposite, and get right into a bad mood. Remind yourself that the world is a grim old place, and people like you never stood a chance. Allow extra time to explore some bitter regrets. Then through gritted teeth, send stress levels skyward again with a fiercely contested commute home.

What's your choice?

Happiness isn't for sale, or guaranteed to appear. We aspire to more, we get more, but still feel bad. So there might be some contradicting messages out there. Happiness is a positive emotional state; therefore unavailable to pre-order or buy.

However we think money can somehow create it. Nope, it just can't. Although money can (as Woody Allen famously said), buy a more comfortable standard of misery.

Neither will happiness be summoned on demand. Yet we feel cheated if it's not there in spades on holiday. Or if it fails to show up on our birthday, or at big family events. If your birthday is full of your sources of happiness – Happy Birthday!

Happiness is feeling, not thinking. So an overly intellectual approach to creating more happiness is a bit like asking your computer for a hug. It doesn't feel that great. Next weekend's diary entry reads, "See friends. Explain logic of why we are friends. Then have fun together". Ah. OK.

Happiness is yours to have here and now, regardless. You being happy doesn't have to be pencilled in for later. If you so decide, it could be now, with everything just as it is. Doesn't have to be when your career/bank account/house value has improved. Your happiness is not dependent on the approval of important people, or money, or deserving it, on account of being a saint.

It simply depends on enough time and room to enjoy your sources of happiness.

Sources could be your closest loving relationships, fulfilling work, time for your own creativity and expression. It could be physical challenge, sport or travel. It could just be time to rest, sleep, chill out and listen to music, to the rain, to the ideas of your friends. Whether you are "a live to work", or a "work to live" person, you still need time to enjoy the sources of your happiness. What did you say yours were again?

- What makes me happy at work?
- At home?
- When do I feel happiest in my own company?
- What will make me happy in the future?

Your Happiness Plan could mean you decide to be as happy as a person can be, sometime this week. They say the best things in life are free. So which do you want?

a) a perfect theory of your future happiness, on ice, ready for the day when you properly deserve it? Or,

b) to walk some of the way home one day this week, see the sky turn gold and red at sunset?

Make it easy. Start with that ABC idea. Allow more room, begin to do things that make you happy and continue. You are the happiness coach in your life, the one who knows best how to design a day-to-day, easy Happiness Plan. Being true to your values, your dreams and your gorgeous uniqueness isn't always easy, especially when there is so much choice, so many ways to go. My advice is to keep it simple.

Remember when I asked you to close your eyes and answer the question, when and where are you happiest? I hope the answer is something to try to do today, and gently, every day.

That's about it. Thank you for reading and I wish you every success with your own Happiness Plan. I hope you enjoy the reading list and the exercises and quizzes (in the next section is a reminder of where they can be found in the book). If you'd like to, please feel free to check out **www.thehappinessplan.com**, for more resources, exercises and ideas.

We're all learning to be happier. Do let me how your Happiness Plan works out via the website, and if you'd like to, just get in touch.

One must practise the things which produce happiness, since if that is present we have everything and if it is absent we do everything in order to have it.

Epicurus

PUT YOUR PLAN INTO ACTION

07

The Happiness Plan steps

STEP 1	Decide to be happier (the ABC approach)
STEP 2	Understand happiness
STEP 3	Create a personal Happiness Plan
STEP 4	Unlearn unhappiness
STEP 5	Our plan. Make others happy
STEP 6	Some Happiness Plan examples
STEP 7	**Put your plan into action**

Thank you for reading the Happiness Plan.

Here is a reminder of some of the exercises, so if you want to structure a seven day Happiness Plan – you can. Hope it helps.

Exercises and Quizzes – Summary

Exercises

Quizzes

HOW CAN YOU BEST USE THE HAPPINESS PLAN?

Suggested Reading

Bunting, Madeleine (2005) *Willing Slaves*, Harper Perennial.

Carson, Rick (2003) *Taming Your Gremlin: A Surprisingly Simple Method for Geting Your Own Way*, Quill.

Ellis, Albert (2006) *How to Stubbornly Refuse to Make Yourself Miserable About Anything*, Citadel Press.

Fisher, Roger and Ury, William (1983) *Getting to Yes*, Arrow Books.

Foster, Rick and Hicks, Greg (1999) *How We Choose to Be Happy*, Prestige Books.

Gilbert, Daniel (2007) *Stumbling on Happiness*, Harper Perennial.

Griffin, Joe and Tyrrell, Ivan (2003) *Human Givens*, HG Publishing.

James, Oliver (2007) *Affluenza*, Random House.

Jeffers, Susan (1991) *Feel the Fear and Do It Anyway*, Arrow Books.

Kets de Vries, Manfred (2001) *The Happiness Equation*, Vermillion.

Lane, Robert E. (2003) *The Loss of Happiness in Market Economies*, Yale University Press.

Layard, Richard (2005) *Happiness: Lessons from a New Science*, Allen Lane.

Neill, Michael (2008) *Feel Happy Now!* Hay House.

Nettle, Daniel (2005) *Happiness*, Oxford University Press.

Persaud, Raj (1997) *Staying Sane*, Bantam Books.

Pink, Daniel (2006) *A Whole New Mind*, Cyan Press.

Ricard, Matthieu (2003) *Happiness – A Guide to Developing Life's Most Important Skill*, Atlantic Books.

Rowe, Dorothy (1996) *Guide to Life*, Harper Perennial.

Scoch, Richard (2007) *The Secrets of Happiness*, Profile Books.

Seligman, Martin E.P. (1991) *Learned Optimism*, Knopf.

Seligman, Martin E.P. (2003) *Authentic Happiness*, Nicholas Brearley.

Walker, Adam (2004) *When Success Is Not Enough*, Piatkus.

Watzlawick, Paul (2003) *The Situation is Hopeless but Not Serious*, Norton Books.

The Happiness Plan Playlist

Thank you for letting me know you enjoyed the playlists in earlier books.

So, from calm to crazy, in roughly that order, here are the tunes that have filled my room with happiness while I've been writing this book.

Song (s)	Artist/Composer
Gymnopedies	Erik Satie
Three little birds	Bob Marley
Autumn in New York	Ella Fitzgerald
Kooks	David Bowie
Let's fall in love	Ella Fitzgerald and Louis Armstrong
Better when we're together	Jack Johnson
Cello Sonata No 3, adagio	Mischa Maisky
Hey Jude	The Beatles
Via con me	Paolo Conte
I was made to love her	Stevie Wonder
Wonderful world	Louis Armstrong
Squares	The Beta Band
Lovecats	The Cure
Brown eyed girl	Van Morrison
Here comes the sun	The Beatles

Song (s)	Artist/Composer
You've got the love	The Source, featuring Candi Staton
Boogie Wonderland	Earth Wind and Fire
Stars	Dubstar
Madame Butterfly	Puccini, sung by Maria Callas
Touch me	The Doors
Crazy	Gnarls Barkley
As	Stevie Wonder song, covered by George Michael and Mary J Blige
Every time I see the girl	Sounds of Eden
No tomorrow	Orson
Dr Pressure	Mylo
I can't wait (for the weekend)	Shapeshifters
Thunderbirds theme	Barry Grey
Hey ya	Outcast
Teenage kicks	The Undertones
H.A.P.P.Y	Edwin Starr